Competitive Cities

Competitive Cities

SUCCEEDING IN THE GLOBAL ECONOMY

Hazel Duffy
Independent writer and consultant
Birmingham, UK

E & FN SPON
An Imprint of Chapman & Hall

London · Glasgow · Weinheim · New York · Tokyo · Melbourne · Madras

Published by E & FN Spon, an imprint of Chapman & Hall, 2–6 Boundary Row, London SE1 8HN, UK

Chapman & Hall, 2–6 Boundary Row, London SE1 8HN, UK
Blackie Academic & Professional, Wester Cleddens Road, Bishopbriggs, Glasgow G64 2NZ, UK
Chapman & Hall GmbH, Pappelallee 3, 69469 Weinheim, Germany
Chapman & Hall USA, 115 Fifth Avenue, New York, NY 10003, USA
Chapman & Hall Japan, ITP-Japan, Kyowa Building, 3F, 2-2-1 Hirakawacho, Chiyoda-ku, Tokyo 102, Japan
Chapman & Hall Australia, 102 Dodds Street, South Melbourne, Victoria 3205, Australia
Chapman & Hall India, R. Seshadri, 32 Second Main Road, CIT East, Madras 600 035, India

First edition 1995

© 1995 Hazel Duffy

Typeset in Times Roman 10/12 by Acorn Bookwork, Salisbury, Wiltshire
Printed in Great Britain by St Edmundsbury Press, Bury St Edmunds, Suffolk

ISBN 0 419 19840 7

A catalogue record for this book is available from the British Library

Library of Congress Catalog Card Number: 95-67607

∞ Printed on permanent acid-free text paper, manufactured in accordance with ANSI/NISO Z39.48-1992 and ANSI/NISO Z39.48-1984 (Permanence of Paper).

To Paul

Contents

Foreword

Within one hundred yards of Harvard's John F. Kennedy School of Government there must be a dozen book stores and perhaps a thousand books on what is wrong with government. It is a shame that there aren't more books about how to fix it.

Hazel Duffy has not written another book for the 'What's Wrong' section. She has written a book for the 'How To' section. It is full of lessons and practical ideas for fixing – or at least rethinking – the way governments work in four big, complex, heavily urbanized regions of Europe and North America. This book ranks right up there with *Reinventing Government* in its usefulness and relevance for people who want to make change in cities. It is not, however, about making bureaucracies work more efficiently, or about restructuring or reorganizing government. It is about the strategies and processes some very different places have employed to try to make themselves both more livable and more competitive in a new global economy. Rather than 'Reinventing government', this book is more about 'Reinventing governance'.

In Atlanta, a city bent on competing better internationally (while at the same time preparing to host a very large international competition!), the critical but not widely understood partnership between business and government is examined for ideas other cities must understand if they are to do more than survive. In the gritty old industrial city of Birmingham, UK, a city council's aggressive economic development strategy offers lessons Detroit, another highly stressed automobile manufacturing center, might profitably examine as it contemplates its own recovery. And in Toronto and Rotterdam, innovation in regional governance and land use planning sets a standard successful cities of the next century must meet if they are to more adequately support their diverse populations, protect their unique environments and assure their economic competitiveness. A premise of this book, therefore, is that the world's cities can learn from each other.

As a former Mayor, I know that to be true. In Seattle we worked at it. In the early eighties we started something called the Intercity Visit. Every year we gathered together a group of civic leaders from both public and private sectors, got on an airplane, and in a tightly planned and organized trip we visited a city which was doing something we thought we could learn from. When we came back we had a larger community discussion about what we had learned and what, as a region, we might do about it. I viewed it as a kind of flying graduate course in urban affairs which also served as a team building device between public and private sectors; a process to help us work better together for the larger community; a way to bridge the distance between business and government, city and suburb, liberal and conservative. We visited Toronto early on, and the last three trips, each involving about one hundred civic leaders, were to Atlanta, Rotterdam and Frankfurt, and the cities of the Kansai Region of Japan (Kobe, Osaka and Kyoto). In each case, our resolve to work together was strengthened by the process, while the work itself was advanced by the new ideas and different perspectives we brought home.

This book springs from a similar examination of six world cities initiated by the German Marshall Fund of the United States, in which a team of journalists and urban experts – including Hazel Duffy – conducted extensive interviews and site visits, and produced a highly readable and sometimes troubling report: *Divided Cities in the Global Economy*. It is striking that the lessons of these very different efforts to understand these places repeat city to city, region to region, country to country: think strategically and regionally, respect, educate and train your workers, maintain a world-class infrastructure, develop partnerships across old political, geographic and philosophical barriers and create solutions that go to your strengths and fit your own traditions and uniquenesses.

Successful cities of the future, both large and small, and regardless of where they are on the world map, must use all their resources if they hope to compete and prosper in a new world economy. In the readable language of an accomplished journalist, this book offers a rich vein of practical, workable ideas from the streets of cities who have realized that and are taking sometimes extraordinary steps to prepare. Movers and shakers, especially in American cities, are well advised to dig them out.

Charles Royer
Seattle, USA

Preface

This book sprang out of a report[1] written as a result of visits to six North Atlantic cities by a small team of journalists and practitioners from both sides of the Atlantic. It was a hopeful report because it concentrated on what cities were doing to help themselves, but it also warned European politicians and communities not to allow their cities to degenerate to the state which was common in too many American cities.

The sponsors of the project were the German Marshall Fund in the United States, which commissions comparative studies of North Atlantic countries, and the participating cities – Frankfurt, Glasgow, Rotterdam, Atlanta, Chicago and Toronto.

Neal Peirce, a journalist and trustee of the Fund, had written 'report cards' on several American cities, which were published in full in the leading newspaper of the city as a popular means of drawing attention to issues. They have now been published in book form.[2] The State-of-the-cities report extended it to Canada and Europe.

Six cities was very ambitious. This book profiles four – Rotterdam, Atlanta, Toronto and Birmingham in the UK, chosen in part because they have a lot in common: racial diversity; unemployment; education and training deficiencies; single-parent and poor families. It seemed like it was always the city that gets the problems and the suburbs that get the gravy.

But each city is much more alive than the problems alone suggest. They look better than they did, they have added new types of jobs and they are bringing more players into the ring. There are plenty of conflicts, but there is a willingness to tackle them in these cities. The book focuses on the actions these cities are taking to make a benefit out of diversity, to treat people as a resource rather than a problem.

The team which produced the report talked with leaders and ideas people. The goal was never to come up with a blueprint, but simply to show what other cities were about, and draw attention to policies and programmes that seemed worth looking at more deeply.

Networks of cities are developing in Europe, like those long established in the United States, and between the continents. But there is always a need for ideas and experience to be swapped. The report tried to fill a little of that gap.

The book looks at some of them in a bit more detail, and how they have fared in the last two years. It also indulges more in the events which helped to shape the cities as they are now: to government in Toronto, the way that politics and business worked in Atlanta, to urban renewal in Rotterdam, and to Birmingham's efforts to make the city more liveable.

The term 'city' is used, rather than city region or city state, but this does not imply that the city is only the buildings and the people within, wherever the limits were drawn.

I thank my colleagues in the Report Card team for some spirited exchanges on cities. We were ably marshalled by Ralph Widner, long-time believer and advocate in the power of cities and regions to achieve the impossible. And I thank all of the people in the cities who gave me time and shared in my enthusiasm for the topic, not least to Professor Alan Middleton, and the library staff, at the University of Central England in Birmingham.

NOTES

1. Report of the 1992 European–North American State-of-the-Cities team (1992) *Divided Cities in the Global Economy*. An initiative of the German Marshall Fund of the United States, co-ordinated by the PSARAS Fund.
2. Peirce, N. R., Johnson, C. W. and Hall, J. S. (1993) *Citistates*, Seven Locks Press, Washington DC.

Introduction

1.1 SIMULATING THE MODEL CITY

Imagine you are the mayor of an embryo city. You have a blank sheet, or in this case a blank screen, on which to divide up the land according to what you want to see happening, whether it be houses, offices or industry. Then it is up to the people who move in to do the building. 'What and how fast they build will depend on how well the omnipotent mayor has thought things out: from public transport to proximity to waterfront or lakeside.'[1] Money must be raised through property taxes. There is an element of fine tuning, since the taxes have to be pitched so that they bring in enough money to finance public services, but are not so high as to discourage people from moving in.

This is SimCity2000, an intelligent, thoroughly addictive, computer game, dreamed up by a bunch of software geniuses in California. It is just one example of the burgeoning demand for entertainment in the form of videos and computer games in the home. As the players sit before their computer screens, they decide that they will enjoy a pizza meal at home. They phone up the local branch of a fast food chain, which is increasingly likely to be part of a multinational group – Pizza Hut, for instance, part of United States-based PepsiCola – which panders ever so slightly to local tastes while reaping economies of scale by centralizing as much as possible of its basic purchases.

The variations on the entertainment theme will multiply as the fruits materialize from the investment that is being poured into the systems and software which bring information, education and entertainment into the home and workplaces, and which allow networks between each of these facilities to be developed. Companies are scurrying to fuse the technical and software elements into a package. In the United States, entertainment and media corporations, including Paramount and CBS, are part of a deadly serious and expensive financial game being played out by the giant telecommunications and cable groups for a place in the future.

A proposed merger between QVC, which launched shopping by television, with CBS, to create a multimedia television programming empire was valued at $7 billion in mid 1994. The deals need know no boundaries. The British-based Pearson group had earlier paid £312m ($462m) for Software Toolworks, an American company specializing in software for personal computers and video-game machines. Microsoft's Bill Gates has warned that multimedia will be a long, very expensive haul. The attraction, however, is the potential of a new global industry. The challenge for the corporate sector is to construct the means at a cost which it can meet.

The risks and rewards of pitching in with new industries are the concerns of the private sector. Kenichi Ohmae, head of McKinsey management consultants in Japan, argued that business was being consumer-driven.

> The pressure of globalization is driven not so much by diversification or competition as by the needs and preferences of customers. Their needs have globalized and the fixed costs of meeting them have soared. That is why we must globalize.[2]

Cities are part of this perspective of a world where national borders are losing significance for producers and consumers, aided by the dismantling of national trade barriers. Jane Jacobs defined the development of cities in terms of their trading histories, and showed how they could grow into mini-economies in their own right.[3] The latter part of the twentieth century has tended to dwell on the threats to city economies from the increasingly international structure of leading manufacturing sectors. Michael Porter, corporate strategist and author of the influential *The Competitive Advantage of Nations*,[4], pointed to the opportunities for cities and regions. He stressed that, far from being smothered by the global economy, authorities had an increasingly important role to play in fostering a local environment where business could flourish.

Porter concluded from his observations of internationally successful industries and industry clusters in several countries, that they

> frequently concentrate in a city or region, and the bases for advantage are often intensely local. Geographic concentration is important to the genesis of competitive advantage and it amplifies the forces that upgrade and sustain advantage. While the national government has a role in upgrading industry, the role of state and local governments is potentially as great or greater.

He gives as examples: university education, infrastructure, local regulations, local research initiatives and information.

'As the borderless and inter-linked economy develops, regional and city-level interests come more and more into play', wrote Kenichi Ohmae from the perspective of the consumer driving the producers. He gave as one example 'informal pairings of cities – not the "sister city" hoopla of boosterism-minded chambers of commerce'[5] but, for instance, the way that Hong Kong capital was moving into Toronto. He argued that this was partly because Canada was one of only two nations to offer Hong Kong nationals the possibility of holding double passports, provided they bring in a certain amount of foreign capital – so there was an important national element – and partly because the city, with its established Chinese community and the infrastructure built up around it, appealed to the Hong Kong national. Ohmae did not mention what is widely perceived in Toronto itself to be part of the attraction to Hong Kong nationals: that Toronto 'works' as a city. It is racially mixed, but it does not have the high crime rate and poor neighbourhoods so often associated with immigration.

Cities are made up of a complex mix of physical, economic and social resources. A successful business sector is only one element. A virile business community in a city does not mean that everybody is provided for, as can be seen in Atlanta. But it is not only the disadvantages brought about by lack of qualifications, for example, that are at stake. The pendulum will swing back in time to knock the business community itself. A city where over one-third of young people leave school poorly equipped for the next stage – and, amazingly, this includes Toronto – will not help its business or its people. This is why parents and business have pushed reform of the management of Chicago schools through the state legislature and why, in Atlanta, the Chamber of Commerce intervened in the city of Atlanta schools by putting up candidates for election to the Board of Education.

Managing a city is actually much more complex than managing a business, as Ohmae concedes. Funding and spending are hedged by restrictions imposed by higher level government, and can be halted by local taxpayers, as in the United States. National and state or provincial governments where appropriate are growing less supportive of cities and their special needs. The Federal budget deficits in the United States and Canada, state and provincial parsimony and national government deficits in Europe, have all conspired to apply pressure for cuts in local social spending. Welfare reform is high on the agenda of every government of the countries whose cities are included in this book. The impact on cities can be most damaging. Tighter restrictions on the individual who can receive unemployment money, for instance, push more people into the lower levels of support. Cities – where unemployment can be twice the national average – are left to pick up the pieces of poverty. Besides, there will always be a proportion of people who, through disability, will not be able to work. Not everybody can be an active worker or self-starter in business.

A well-run city tries to provide for all of its citizens, not only those who will prosper with the consolidation and growth of business in the region. The problems multiply, of course, when those in need become concentrated in certain districts, and there is no mechanism to make the wealthier parts of the area around the city pay towards the costs of special needs. In fact, newer suburbs tend to resist being dragged into what they see as city problems. Meanwhile, local government bureaucrats are being pushed into behaving more like corporate managers, while still being steered by politicians who have economic, social and even racial agendas which do not necessarily coincide with the dominant needs of the established business community.

There are no simple solutions, but cities cannot afford to ignore what is happening in the economy at large. As the barriers to free trade come down, not only within free trade areas like the European Union and North America but also between free trade areas and in the world at large, the need to consolidate the competitive advantages becomes even greater. Cities have been in the front line of manufacturing industries' restructuring. Services sometimes fared almost as badly in the recession that gripped each country in the early 1990s. Even financial services have not been immune to job cuts brought about in response to increased competition – Toronto lost around 6000 jobs in financial services in one year.

Jobs were the most pressing issue cited in dozens of interviews in the public and private sectors in each of the cities in this book: how to create and sustain an employment base which will provide middle- and high-income jobs, and give employment to school-leavers who will not go on to higher education. The goal is job creation. Most cities have concluded that they must win inward investment in addition to promoting self-gen-erated growth. Jobs have been disappearing faster than they have been appearing in the industrial cities across northern Europe and North America. Birmingham lost nearly 60 000 jobs between 1981 and 1992, a drop of 11.2% in employment. In comparison, its region, the West Mid-lands, lost just 0.7% while, nationally, Britain increased employment by 5% in the same period.

The prospect of inward investment from other parts of the country and from overseas has put cities, more than ever, into a sort of beauty parade. They must give prospective investors a panoply of reasons why a company should choose that particular location for the branch plant, head office, regional office, or simply back office which will employ hun-dreds of low-paid, often part-time data processors. They point to the cul-tural pursuits of the city, shopping facilities, public transport, sporting features and ease of access to the pleasant suburbs and villages beyond the city where the managers can decide to live, as well as to the skills and education of the people. Specifically, they parade the sites to be made available for offices and manufacturing. Finally, in some cities, there is the prospect of grants to help the investor make the final decision.

Weighing up the options

David Harvey, one of the leading urban geographers, proffered the advice in the late 1980s that 'those urban regions that achieve a superior competitive position survive, at least in the short run, and do better than those that do not'. In the face of the international division of labour, he listed options for the authorities:

> improved infrastructures; close attention to the productive forces embedded in the land (water, sewage, and so forth) . . . investments in social infrastructures – education, science and technology – that improve the urban climate as a centre of innovation.

Cities might approach the problem from the perspective of 'the spatial division of consumption' – and invest in a 'good living environment'. This is expensive, and it is high-risk, but if the city turns out to be one of the successes, the pay-off can be attractive. Cities might also decide to compete for 'key control and command functions in high finance and government'. Again, this is playing for high stakes. The incumbent cities are not likely to relax their hold on the institutions of government and finance.

Or they might pitch for the 'redistribution of economic power' at the national level – making sure of a designation which allows the offer of grants to investors, bidding for defence institutions, or other categories of spending initiated by the higher levels of government.[6]

Clearing the way

In the main, local authorities can only prepare the ground for private enterprise. There have been examples in the past of government intervening in the local economy, by investing in companies, either to propel their progress, or to rescue them when in trouble. Generally, this is not now an option open to local government. There are exceptions, such as in Rotterdam, where taking an equity stake in ventures might be possible for the development corporation. This is different from the cases where councils have set up companies to run dedicated public facilities like airports, ports or convention centres.

The public authorities of the cities in this book, in practice, have tried to do a little of everything: get grants status to attract outsider companies; make the city centres look more attractive; add a bit to government training money. Few cities had the confidence to go single-mindedly down one route.

Climbing the charts

Each city is a 'second city' in the sense that none is a capital city. However, the Greater Toronto Area, with a population of 5 million, is the dominant urban region in Canada. Rotterdam and the other cities in the Randstad (Amsterdam, The Hague and Utrecht) form the main urban area of the Netherlands. While not world cities, in terms of their functional significance and the areas over which their influence extends, these four are firmly in the second tier of European cities. Birmingham calls itself the second city in Britain, but it is classified by DATAR (France's inward investment agency) below Manchester, always its rival for 'second city' status in Britain. Atlanta, meanwhile, is dominant within a 60-mile radius, while at the same time, taking into account its airport, corporate head and regional offices, it claims itself the 'undisputed capital' of the south-east United States.

At various times, politicians like to think that their cities will be, or are, 'international' or 'world' cities – a mysterious goal in the sense that there is no accepted definition of the qualifications needed. At one level, Birmingham has already been there. It was one of five British cities which ranked in the top 19 world cities in 1900, all of them connected to the 'world economy' in general, and specifically in the case of the British cities, to a colonial mode of production.[7] Local politicians today cite physical facilities, like an international airport, as qualification. Geographers put it rather differently: a city would need to be 'a basing point in the spatial organization and articulation of production and markets'.[8] This was one of several hypotheses formulated by Friedmann in linking international economic developments with urbanization. Taking New York, London and Tokyo as 'global' cities, a series of 'second-tier' world cities follows that could include Chicago, Los Angeles, Frankfurt, Paris, Berlin, Milan, Osaka and Nagoya. In terms of the concentration of capital, in financial markets, banking and the growth of trading companies whose tentacles spread increasingly into the United States, Toronto 'could be brought up to this tier'.[9] Rotterdam, meanwhile, is most heavily involved in international shipping and transport; Atlanta is trying hardest to climb up the international ladder; Birmingham has most aggressively bought and used culture to gain international recognition.

The possibilities and the problems: the four cities

Birmingham:
Is in the heart of the West Midlands, Britain's most diverse manufacturing region. Over the last decade, the West Midlands was highly successful in attracting overseas manufacturing investment, both to greenfield sites in the new towns, or designated development areas, like Telford and Red-

ditch, and those of its companies taken over by foreign buyers. Yet the region suffered the steepest proportionate decline of any part of Britain in manufacturing jobs in the early 1980s, and again was caught in a phase of thorough corporate restructuring especially between 1990 and 1993. In both periods, the manufacturing base of Britain shrank dramatically. All of this had its effect on the metropolitan area of Birmingham.

But the region still has considerable strengths, albeit concentrated to some extent in sectors which still face further contraction on the European scale. Vehicle makers include Rover and Land Rover, owned by BMW of Germany since early 1994, and Jaguar, which is part of Ford. Ownership of automotive components manufacturers in the area resides in the United States, Germany and Japan as well as Britain. Some 80% of components production is exported, in part or in the final product. They are sophisticated and they are more basic. This geographic concentration in engineering is characterized by the sort of supplier base in processes like forging, pressing and stamping, and products like industrial fasteners on which the larger sector depends – suppliers at this level tend to be more localized. To this extent, and with the sophisticated buyers either in or within easy access of the area, Birmingham and the conurbation measures up to some of the demanding criteria that Porter sets for there to be competitive advantage. New firms are not, however, being formed in this sector in the main, despite good access in the area to venture capital for developing companies. Some metal treatment processes will have great difficulty in complying with environmental standards laid down by the European Union. These companies seem most likely to die out. In general, investment in equipment and people by companies in the West Midlands has been inadequate to sustain an expanding base in the highly competitive engineering sector, spelling continued uncertainty over its future.

Birmingham itself has consolidated its position as the source of services to business, such as accounting, consulting, advertising and legal services, within the region. With exceptions, it has not expanded the provision of services beyond the region. The health of its services sector is broadly dependent on activity levels in manufacturing. The city's financial support of cultural development has not so far materially changed its image nationally of a grimy, industrial city. Consumers in the wealthy semi-rural hinterland prefer to shop elsewhere. Highly qualified, potential high income earners in Britain and continental Europe are rarely attracted to the city. It remains a city to which people are unlikely to want to move out of choice. This is an indication of the dogged determination needed by the authorities if they are going to change its image.

Rotterdam:
Starts with the competitive advantage of the unique factor, in Porter terminology, of its location, which gave it its port. The activities in and

around the port are an important component in the Netherlands' exports. The port has automated much of its handling, with the result that thousands of workers were no longer needed. Investment in logistics to control movements of ships and goods within the port have made it safer as well as more efficient. Porter's maxim to companies applies to the port: competitive advantage 'grows fundamentally out of improvement, innovation and change . . . [it] is sustained only through relentless improvement'.[10]

The cost base of the port, which is owned by the city, is still too high in relation to the competition, say employers, who want port workers to agree to more flexible working conditions. A long-term investment plan has been agreed between the city and trade unions and other groups to upgrade facilities. The national government is starting to support new infrastructure projects which will enhance the competitiveness of the port in relation to its customers throughout Europe. Infrastructure in itself is rarely a source of industrial competitive advantage, but it can well be a disadvantage if it is not upgraded, according to Porter. Land use in the Rotterdam area, however, will always be controversial, given the restrictions on physical expansion in the Randstad.

Another 'advanced competitive factor', as Porter would see it, lies in the highly specialized skills of people employed in the port area to handle petrochemicals and chemicals. By encouraging geographically concentrated clusters, the port economy is far better than if it had tried to foster diverse and random groups of industries. Nevertheless, the authorities are actively encouraging more diversity by trying to attract more process industries to the port area – for example, certain types of food and drink, and highly specialized chemicals – based on the products which go through the port.

The city's services sector includes the head offices of Robeco, an international investment fund, and ING, one of the big Dutch banking groups, the Dutch part of Anglo-Dutch Unilever, as well as transport and shipping groups based on the port. The electronics industry is well represented. But more jobs and training opportunities must be sought if the unemployment rate, pushing well above 20% in 1994, is to be brought down. Unemployment is seen by the authorities as the city's major problem.

Toronto:

The wider Toronto area has grown rapidly in population and employment during the last 30 years, but the steep decline in manufacturing since the 1980s, in response to restructuring by multinational companies and their suppliers, and the onset of the free trade agreement with the United States, has left a jobs gap among older and less educated people. The abrupt end in early 1990 to the long period of prosperity shocked a population which had grown accustomed to growth. The basis for the recession was ascribed to an over-geared property sector and the adjustment of an often complacent manufacturing sector, cosseted by protective barriers. The free trade agreement which later brought in Mexico was the catalyst for change, although the devaluation of the Canadian dollar brought costs more into line – and made manufacturing more competitive – with the United States.

Toronto has enhanced its competitiveness in certain service areas, particularly banking, where it has benefited from uncertainties over the future status of Quebec and stolen a march on Montreal, a rival banking centre. The city has attracted foreign banks and security houses since deregulation of financial services in 1987. The stock market is Canada's largest, and used as the base for the rapidly growing trading in option products.

Canada's relations with business in the United States are growing less dependent and more resourceful. But the implications of this more thrusting managerial stance for Toronto, which has been able to avoid the economic and social polarization of American cities, will become more apparent by the end of the decade. But perhaps the most serious effect on Toronto's stable social and racial make-up will be the pulling back by federal and provincial governments which in the past have helped manage the rapid growth of the city.

Atlanta:
In one of the growth areas in the United States over the last 20 years, is an aggressive pursuer of inward investment. Climate and a reputation for harmonious race relations have enhanced its attractions to migrants from the northern United States. Asian and Hispanic immigration is expanding from a small base. The basis of the Atlanta economy is that job creation equals workforce growth, which leads to economic growth. The range of imported skills has helped to buoy up an area where educational achievement is low. But poverty and social problems in the City of Atlanta and inner suburbs could puncture the buoyant image.

The best known home-grown corporation is the Coca-Cola Company – the drink was first served up in a drug store in the city over a hundred years ago – which flourishes on the sort of domestic competitive rivalry between companies that Porter identified as an advantage. It has also made a significant contribution as one of the core of downtown companies which had informal working relationships with politicians in the city. The city's successful bid to stage the 1996 Olympic Games made evident this partnership between business and politics. Although the allocation of responsibilities is not always as straightforward as the reputation suggests, this is still a city which is an advertisement for the sort of partnership that others are building hesitantly.

Continued dependence on the import of jobs as the means to sustain growth, however, is questioned in some quarters. The core of companies in telecommunications, cable and media suggests more concentration on growth areas as one objective. Upgrading of traditional industries by introducing advanced technologies – another Porter recommendation – is another. Atlanta also needs to create a social and administrative cohesion between the expanding suburbs and the city, not least in reconciling issues of car use and the environment.

Who manages?

Each one of these four cities is juggling with the effects of changes in the economy, and changes in the social structure. The city bureaucrats are not the ideal material to manage change. They do not have the freedom that is open to company managers. But the public sector has sometimes had the innovative edge over business. Cities have to think more in terms of co-operation. Partnership has been a traditional description of the dependence on each other of planning and property development. Increasingly, however, simply to set out plans and wait for the developers to come along is not enough. Cities have had to kick-start the process in those districts on which developers turn their backs, by buying up land, putting together a portfolio of property ready to attract outsiders; innovative financial packages have been drawn up to finance the properties that they hope will bring a sparkle to the eyes of the property investors.

Some sort of partnership arrangement is increasingly being pushed on local government and business by central and state governments wanting to cut their social services spending. At this stage, it is unclear that business is suited to take on anti-poverty programmes, for instance, although business leaders are more relaxed about partnership arrangements in training and education. But even these agreements can sometimes get entangled in a web of bureaucracy which ultimately discourages the business leaders.

Bureaucrats need to be more open, more sensitive to fresh ideas. Often there is a reluctance to embrace ideas suggested by outsiders. Robert Reich (now President Clinton's Labour Secretary) found business looking for 'strategic brokers' – people who are 'continuously engaged in managing ideas' rather than 'controlling organisations, founding businesses, or inventing things'.[11] They might well be floaters – unattached to any one employer for any length of time. Likewise with city managers. They need ideas, new ways of thinking if cities are not all to take too similar paths.

The progress of the city is tied up with its ability to provide better care for those who are too old or disabled to work, for parents to bring up children in safer and more congenial environments. Equally it should be tied up more than it is with 'sustainable' growth pledges made by their governments at the Rio environment summit.

Winning a head office relocation does not contribute to a better environment unless it gives at least a chance to the people whose confidence about work has been blunted by long spells of unemployment. Toronto has demonstrated that a moderate degree of social equity is positively to its advantage. But the investors, who can pick and choose between countries and locations within that country, can make heavy demands on their suitors.

Inward investors are very demanding of both the working and physical environment in which they locate. The strategic question for cities like Birmingham is: how far are they prepared to go to join that very fast track competition? In fact there are quite a lot of cities with advantages which we cannot replicate. Assuming that most cities are not going to be successful, what does it say about social welfare and employment issues for the vast majority? Can they at that stage turn minds to other ways of keeping people occupied and rewarded which do not fall within the normal compass of economic activity?[12]

1.2 WHAT MOST CITIES HAVE TO SHARE

Decline of industry

The decline in industrial jobs has had a profound effect on all western economies. Starting with the oil price crisis in 1973, industry in North America and Europe had entered on a long phase of girding itself to compete with the economies of the countries in the Far East, first Japan, then Korea, Taiwan, and now a new generation of companies which have matured in the Pacific Rim. Unemployment in the OECD doubled between 1974 and the end of the decade to 20 million. The recession in 1980–81 pushed the number up to 23 million by 1981. In 1994 it was 35 million.

The vulnerability of manufacturing to new competitors, new products, new methods of manufacture, is certainly not a phenomenon of the twentieth century. Birmingham was a good example. In the eighteenth century it started out making harnesses, horse brasses and buckles. As different products were invented, Birmingham made them. The old products did not disappear but moved somewhere else. Walsall, one of the towns adjacent to Birmingham, still makes horse saddlery.

In Canada, Toronto grew with the exploitation of the forests and minerals in the interior. Both helped to establish Toronto as a trading city, and a port whence timber was shipped to Europe. South American forests opened up, and Ontario had to find new activities. Toronto, meanwhile, built on the commercial and trading skills which were the residue of the timber-broking days.

The scale of manufacturing decline that followed the shift in the balance of economic power between the oil producers in OPEC and the big consumer countries in the 1970s and 1980s, however, was something for which governments were quite unprepared. The impact was most severe in areas dependent on single industries. The steel closures in Sheffield, for example, had a dramatic effect on the whole city. In the mid-1980s it was hard to find any job in the city no matter what your qualifications and experience. Likewise on Teesside when jobs in the big chemicals plants were rationalized. The jobs that went left a big hole. They had usually been well paid, and companies had trained young men for work which they expected to do until they were 65.

The collapse was not confined to industrial cities. The greatest proportional loss was sometimes in capital cities. Manufacturing employment in London declined by half in the shake-out which culminated in the recession of 1980–1, against a little over 40% in the industrial conurbations. In cities across the United States, manufacturing jobs disappeared. In Chicago, manufacturing had accounted for 45% of jobs in 1963. By 1985, it was down to 20%. In the Great Lakes region, the fall was less severe – between 1963 and 1989 a decline of 6% – but this needed to be seen in relation to an increase of 14% in manufacturing jobs across the country as a whole. Chicago suffered from the 'decentralization' described below; the Great Lakes area, meanwhile, suffered from the shift in manufacturing to other parts of the country.

Across the Great Lakes into Canada, Toronto, like Chicago, had a traditionally strong but declining manufacturing base. Manufacturing employment was down to 18% of the total workforce in 1991. In that city, the early 1990s recession turned out to be more severe than that 10 years earlier. Unemployment rose for nearly three years. Almost all cities had an important employment component in manufacturing, even if it had not been the strongest reason for its growth.

Distribution was Atlanta's original reason for existence. But manufacturing developed as an important wing of the economy – until rationalization. Lockheed Aircraft laid off 10 000 workers in the late 1980s, over half of the 18 000 manufacturing jobs overall which went in the region, although it has since taken workers back. As a proportion of total employment, manufacturing fell from 14.9% in 1980 to 10.7% ten years later.

Not all of the plants which closed had reached the end of their useful life. City-located plants might be the beneficiaries of investment one year and yet still close the next year as group managers chased the maximization of margins to be gained from relocation. Without changes in labour practices, capital investment in itself did not bring about the required returns. Costs were the significant factor. The automotive industry in Southern Ontario was one example. The United States-based car and vehicle makers rationalized production and closed some plants, but invested in others to make them much more competitive.

New and more sophisticated engineering technologies and techniques developed rapidly during the 1980s, often under Japanese inspiration, transforming not only the manning of assembly lines for volume production but also making possible reductions in skilled labour in batch production. The driving forces are the need to satisfy the customers' desire for variations of standard models, higher standards of quality and reliability, and diminishing costs. The results frequently brought job losses and the movement of large-scale manufacturing out of the city. In addition, labour-intensive sectors which had always been an integral part of the city employment pattern, like clothing, tobacco, food and drink, and printing, also shed jobs.

Leaving the city: business

People and jobs have been leaving the city for decades. The big exodus to the suburbs of American and British cities goes back to the 1930s. North European cities saw another wave follow in the 1960s, partly as a result of large-scale clearance of bad housing – slum clearance – when families were rehoused both in new towns and 'overspill' areas in the suburbs, as well as in redeveloped areas of the cities. The move to new towns built in mostly rural areas was deemed a healthy process in every respect. The families who moved, however, tended to have a head of household with skills. Only much later did the effect of this creaming process on the structure of the city population become apparent. This was also the period when the middle classes left cities to settle in areas where they could buy and rent single houses which were unavailable in the city – as in Rotterdam – hastening what has been referred to as 'the pauperization of the city'.

Meanwhile, in industry, companies wanted space to expand. Changes in manufacturing technologies in part led to companies needing bigger plants and space to expand. They left the hemmed-in city cores for the outer suburbs and beyond. The more far-flung locations became realistic with the development of motorway networks. The construction cost of these networks was not fully reflected in road taxes. There was another advantage to be gained from placing plants away from the city: access by trucks, both delivering materials and parts and picking up the product, was easier and more reliable than the often tortuous street networks of a city. Only later did official consideration respond to the business need for better internal city road systems to facilitate access to sites. The cost, however, of building roads in such areas is enormous. Where they had been occupied by industries and utilities which left the ground heavily polluted, and where remaining companies are removed, with compensation, to make way for mixed use of the land, the procedure is laborious as well as expensive. The upgrading of infrastructure in inner city areas is obviously much more costly than on open land that has not been used by industry.

It is not only manufacturing which has been moving out from the cities. The just-in-time technique which cuts inventory costs for the end-product maker has spawned the growth of distribution centres. So has the growth in variety of foodstuffs stocked by supermarket chains. National and regional distribution centres catering to these needs can equally well be located in semi-rural areas as close to cities, provided the delivery vehicles can quickly reach the motorways.

The patterns of relocation of manufacturing from the city core have been determined increasingly by ease and cost of transportation. New locations might be 50 or more miles from the city in North America, while still being within the 'urban field'.[13] Nelson demonstrated that, partly because of the census classifications, the extent of industrialization in the areas which span 'urban/suburban areas and the truly rural land-scape', exurban growth had been underestimated. His findings showed that overall employment in exurban counties rose by 85% between 1965 and 1985, and that manufacturing employment, which went up by 31%, was the 'largest nominal increase in manufacturing jobs among all spatial types during this period'.

Studies in Britain in the early 1980s suggested that lack of space rather than labour supply factors was the prime reason for decentralization and the urban–rural shift in growth rates of manufacturing employment.[14]

In the United States and Canada, growth centres are often located where two main highways intersect. Atlanta is a good example. Most of the commercial development and population growth has been to the north-east and north-west of the city, along highways 75 and 85. The far commuting arc stretches into the north of Georgia and eastern Alabama.

But the trend is not solely for all types of business to move ever further out. Offices in suburban Atlanta developed rapidly in the 1980s at the expense of the central city. The growth points at the intersections of the main highways and the urban route due north, were dubbed 'urban vil-lages'[15] by the authors who observed that urban areas no longer grew *around* the city core, but spread out from a series of new suburban cores each with its own spheres of influence. They pointed out that not only sunbelt cities like Atlanta had developed like this, but also 'slow-growing older ones like St. Louis and Kansas City, and archetypal cities like New York and Baltimore'. More recently, the term 'edge city' has become popular. It means new towering office blocks and campus style business parks. At least 5 million sq. ft of office space is needed to earn the edge city accolade, since this amount provides the impetus for more development. It means new shopping, entertainment and residential development, where just 30 years ago there would have been only a dor-mitory suburb, or even open land.[16] Edge cities are as familiar in Canada as in the United States. Markham, in the Toronto area, is an example referred to later. One review of Garreau's work on edge cities suggested that: 'the move is on to Nowheresville USA.'

In European urban areas, the spread of population and employment is hindered more than in North America by stricter planning controls, not least by green rings around continental European cities and green belts around major British cities. Urban sprawl, however, is no stranger to industrial Europe. The Birmingham/Black Country conurbation is an unrelieved spread of industry and housing which stretches 23 miles from the suburb of Solihull to the town of Wolverhampton.

Development has jumped the green belts in Britain, particularly in the south-east of England where the fastest growing towns in population terms are located west of London along the M4 corridor, within reach of London Heathrow airport. Even so, there have been incursions into the green belts. Inward investors in particular seem uninterested in urban sites – this is common to each of the areas studied in this book – and controls can be relaxed when the lure of new jobs is stronger than environmental will.

Intense pressure has been put on the authorities by developers in Britain to release more sites in the green belt both for housing and for business parks suitable to a wide range of offices. As in North America, most new shopping development in Britain in recent years has been outside the city, close to major highways. The national government having permitted between 1986 and 1990 several major shopping centre developments – it has the final say on such plans – in 1994 went into reverse and decided that town 'high streets' were indeed suffering as a result of these out-of-town shopping emporia. The line on planning permissions would be tougher in future, it pronounced. One of the most potent examples is in the West Midlands, in the town of Dudley, from where most big retail chains have departed for a big shopping centre, Merry Hill, located on the site of a former steelworks. Like others in Britain, the financing was subsidized by government with substantial tax concessions to the developers.

In the west of the Netherlands, where the major business and population centres are located, the cities of Amsterdam, Rotterdam, The Hague and Utrecht circle a 'green heart'. Like the green belts in Britain, the green heart as a place for leisure is a valuable advantage in the region's competitiveness, so long as it can be maintained. Pressure is growing for more new housing and improved infrastructure, which will have to be carefully planned to avoid eating into the heart.

Leaving the city: population

In the United States, city cores generally lost population and employment from the 1950s and 1960s, a pattern repeated a decade later in many European cities. The Toronto metropolitan area, however, which includes the

City of Toronto and five suburban authorities with populations ranging from nearly 100 000 to 542 000, has stabilized rather than lost population.

The steepest population losses have been from inner areas, some of them adjacent to city centres. In these districts, housing and workplaces were cleared, sometimes in favour of lower-density high income housing, but more often to be replaced by public sector housing, highways, and public amenities, like sports stadia. Working-class areas of cities like Birmingham and Rotterdam were densely populated before redevelopment. Even when districts have been refurbished rather than cleared, the densities could not be maintained.

Over the last decade, however, many cities have seen a slight reversal of the downward trend. In the United States, metropolitan areas as defined for census purposes, broader than the city itself, found population growing slightly during the 1980s. This prompted commentators to talk of urban revival in contrast to the 'counter-urbanization' which marked the 1970s. In the core city, redeveloped districts around the centre and restored waterfronts, for instance, have included housing in a deliberate attempt by the local authorities to tempt the middle classes back to city residence. Even with authorities previously hostile to inner city housing, on the basis that business use provided a stronger tax base than residential use, the mood has changed. This trickle back has been most pronounced among young people, and couples whose families have grown up, but it should not be put out of proportion.

> 'Yuppies' and the upper middle class cannot sustain a regeneration of the cities. The well-to-do are relatively few in number, while many young workers will move to the suburbs once they have families and school-age children.[17]

The paper argued for a programme of 'fiscal equalization that creates a "more level playing field" between city and suburb in terms of tax rates and the cost of local public services'. City authorities which encouraged experiments in private developments of affordable housing in the inner areas – they include Birmingham and Rotterdam – have found them to be in demand. Poor standards in education in inner city schools, however, deter families.

Decentralization does not have to be a threat to the health of the city proper as long as the authorities can plan and sustain a new mix of functions in the place of the departed department stores and bank head offices.

> There are lessons for cities from biology. Other things being equal, a diverse population is more likely to survive perilous change than a homogenous population – because a diverse population is more likely

to contain individuals that breed under the new circumstances. Likewise, cities and parts of cities that contain a mix of uses may be more likely to thrive during change. Thus, as far as possible, we should avoid concentrations of single uses, whether downtown or in the suburbs.[18]

Holding the centre

Getting the development balance right between the central city and outside is one of the most important issues in urban planning. Office and shop rents in the centre tend to be higher than in the suburbs and on the periphery. They can be relatively high in inner areas as well, in part because the users are sometimes on the point of being forced out: for this they will be compensated and the rents can reflect this expectation. The activities of public authorities in buying and selling land in such areas to encourage redevelopment can create an inflated market price where none had existed.

The sad, empty department stores in central streets, like Rich's in downtown Atlanta, Lewis's in central Birmingham, need not be a disaster for the city if the buildings are quickly put to other productive uses. The public sector must usually take the lead as tenants. The refurbished Birmingham building, in fact, will open shortly as offices for the regional law courts, the state thus using its own requirements to underpin the financial risk of the private sector developer. The regional offices of Coopers & Lybrand, consultants and accountants, will also be in the block. The plan to transform the former Rich's store into offices for the Federal government in Atlanta has similarities. The new uses thereby emphasize the continuing role of these cities as regional centres for public and private interests.

City centre redevelopment of the past decade emphasized the resurgence of the private sector in the development process. Within that relatively short period, the centres of many North American cities were transformed into towers of glass-fronted offices. The private corporations which stayed downtown have also been concerned to maintain the value of their investments. The concerted effort by the big downtown corporations in Atlanta to hold the centre in the face of departing business, and the arrival of new companies in the suburbs, is one of the most fascinating studies of private influence on public policy. In Atlanta, the redevelopment of the city end of Peachtree Street in the early 1970s was an example of the private sector, with the aid of public subsidies, holding in check the threatened decline of the district. The superstructure for the 1996 Olympics will be used in a similar vein. The growing dominance from the 1970s of Toronto as Canada's financial centre spurred an explosion of new downtown high-rise offices. But the city's authorities also initiated flagship developments to revive the areas adjacent to the business district, with hotels, the opening of the waterfront and the SkyDome stadium; all attracted a mixture of public and private finance. The waterfront, which had the greatest potential, has been the least successful in obtaining a good mix of public and private uses, the balance having been permitted to sway too much to luxury residential.

In Europe, the developers and investors were more cautious, at least in the second-tier cities. Indeed, the emphasis has been on enhancement rather than transformation. Many borrowed from the American flagship examples to stimulate private investment. The configuration in the redeveloped Waterstad part of Rotterdam, however, was more public than private, led by the siting of the Maritime Museum and the construction of exciting cube-style housing. But the authorities here were dipping a cautious toe in the waters to test how much the private sector would follow. The new development area on the south bank, initiated by big spending on infrastructure and anchored by government tenants, will draw in a much higher proportion of private finance, or so the Rotterdam authorities hope.

Birmingham's flagship developments came too late to catch the surge in property values between 1987 and 1990, although there was a modest amount of new office space coming on stream in the more traditional commercial areas during that period. But by 1993–94, there were signs that investors were beginning to renew their interest. Their response will be critical to the overall success of ambitions to break the narrow city centre out of its road-defined tight boundaries.

Running the city with the region

Many functions in the city cannot be performed effectively on the basis of the city as defined by its administrative limits. The city still exercises an influence and acts as the focal point for key economic activities, like business services, while its attractions as the centre for cultural, educational and health activities affect a much wider area. It can be argued that the influence of the city is no longer pre-eminent, but simply one of many centres scattered around the metropolitan area. But, even in Atlanta, where urban villages and edge cities abound, it is in the city that most of the Olympics events will be staged, that is the destination for visitors flocking to watch major league baseball and football, and that houses the State capitol and the concentration of facilities like luxury hotels. Hartsfield International airport, meanwhile, serves as the premier hub for a region of 40 million people.

The administrative size of the city does not necessarily correspond to its sphere of influence. In the United States the boundaries of the original cities have mostly not been extended for several decades. In many big urban areas the administrative city now comprises perhaps only one-quarter of the metropolitan area. The exodus of people and business to the suburbs eroded the financial base of many large cities in the 1960s and 1970s, reducing some to virtual bankruptcy, New York included. The business tax base of these cities then received a huge boost in the 1980s with the central city a focus for a new burst of property development. Still, the plight of the inner areas continues to emphasize the imbalance between needs and the ability to raise money to meet them. This does not mean that the suburbs are without needs. The independent Atlanta Project, for instance, which was formed in 1992 to fight the spreading poverty and crime in the city, spills over the city boundaries. Levels of achievement in schools outside the city, which are the responsibility of the state, are sometimes poorer than in the city.

Metropolitan areas across America are handicapped by the scant official procedures to equalize revenues and spending needs between municipalities, or, for that matter, between states. In the absence of reform of local government – many cities are actually creatures of their states, allowed to engage only in activities permitted by the state – a proliferation of special bodies, elected and non-elected, has grown up to provide services across the administrative boundaries.

Of course, there is some co-operation among these proliferating organizations. Indeed, the Federal government has imposed an obligation to plan on a regional basis. But the degree to which this requirement is carried out differs from one area to another. To Europeans, and indeed some Americans, this is a crass way of going on. Metropolitan government, or government of a territory analogous to the city-region has been advocated as the solution. But the topic of territorial boundaries has not gripped Americans. Rather, the inefficiencies of government, contrasted with the rigorous cost-cutting exercises of business, have been the dominant preoccupation. The way in which local government has been administered – and not only in cities – is to

> focus on inputs, not outcomes. They fund schools based on how many children enroll; welfare based on how many poor people are eligible; police departments based on police estimates of manpower needed to fight crime. They pay little attention to outcomes – to **results**. It doesn't matter how well the children do in one school versus another, how many poor people get off welfare into stable jobs, how much the crime rate falls or how secure the public feels.[19]

The budget performance of city halls in some big American cities – helped by the more buoyant business tax base – has improved immeasurably in the last decade, Philadelphia being the latest near casualty seemingly to have got into the recovery league under the leadership of a new mayor.

Politicians have started to grasp the nettle of inflated administration costs. The finances of the City of Atlanta seemed to be worsening however, with capital spending and maintenance demands soaring. The City wanted voters to agree a special tax to pay for essential repairs only months after the new mayor – whose campaign said that tax increases were not necessary – had taken office.

Local government in Canada is the creature of the province which has a more powerful role than the American state. In the case of Toronto, the province of Ontario supported the city. Toronto's public services were among the best of any city in North America. But the need for its two-tier system of administration has been questioned more by taxpayers in the last few years. The higher rate of taxation within the city boundaries than outside has been put under the spotlight by businesses who examine every cost in the more exposed climate that free trade has ushered in. It is not really possible to quantify the contribution of government to the long period of economic growth and social stability that Toronto has enjoyed. But it has been a more positive influence than it is getting credit for in some quarters. It did owe a lot to the time when the province viewed the city as an engine of growth in the region, and to the system of sharing revenues between authorities to meet their requirements.

The province's failure was not to extend the boundaries of government as the city expanded. Toronto in the 1990s is increasingly having to seek a means of co-operating with neighbouring municipalities, setting up joint non-elected boards of administration similar to the systems pioneered by American non-elected regional authorities. The tax variation between metropolitan and outer suburban areas is also very similar to that between American cities and their suburbs. The inner ring of suburbs within metropolitan Toronto could feel the effects if there is not a resolution of the tax differential and the system of tax assessment.

Britain, unlike Germany, and France since 1982, does not have elected governments in the regions. Government of the big cities has been through the creation of metropolitan government and then its abolition within the space of 15 years. More significant than the boundaries, however, has been the diminution of local government's powers of control in key services in favour of the centre. Scotland had a different system, with regional councils, which took in urban and rural areas, but by 1994 this too was being dismantled. The big city authorities like Birmingham were given key services like education when the metropolitan counties disappeared, only to have the allocation of responsibility shaken up again. Schools are invited to leave local authority control and act autonomously, drawing their funding from the national government. Further education colleges, until recently funded by local government, are now financed by a non-elected body at the centre.

So it is a very mixed picture that emerges of local government in

Britain. Physical and economic planning at the sub-regional and regional levels takes place within non-elected, low-profile fora. Critics of the present system, most particularly as it left London without any elected body for the capital as a whole, point to the difficulties of securing agreement on planning matters that span several authorities. Another bout of change has been foreshadowed by the government which favours single-tier local authorities. If implemented – and there have been doubts about how far-ranging would be any further change – it would tend to give more power to smaller cities. The large metropolitan areas would not be involved.

The Netherlands, on the other hand, is planning, theoretically at least, to devolve power to new elected authorities which broadly correspond to the metropolitan areas of Amsterdam, Rotterdam and other cities. But this will not be an additional tier. The present provincial tier will go. In the Rotterdam area, the city council will also be dissolved, by its own volition, in a bid to make the new system work. Politicians argued that its continuation would have meant that, by virtue of its size, it would dominate the new structure, to the detriment of the whole. The Netherlands, traditionally highly centralized, will be watched with interest in most of Europe and North America. At this stage, there are critics as well as enthusiasts. 'Here one sees proposals for strong unitary administration at the city-regional level, without sufficient guarantees for competition, besides co-operation, between the municipalities within the city region'.[20] Others say that success will depend on central government being prepared to part with power and finance, or warn that the disappearance of the city of Rotterdam will weaken the administrative system which has avoided extremes of wealth and poverty in the cities.

Euro-Funds to the rescue?

From the start of the European Economic Community in 1957, governments expressed their anxiety 'to ensure their harmonious development by reducing the differences existing between the various regions'.[21] They set up the European Regional Development Fund in 1975. But the amounts of money it disbursed have never done more than ameleriorate the relative differences between regional economies. The lion's share of funding has gone to the predominantly rural underdeveloped areas of Greece, Ireland, Portugal, Spain and south Italy. During the 1980s, however, areas – often amounting to sub-regions – which had been hit by industrial decline in the wealthier states became eligible for assistance. Especially from 1988, cities started to creep into the funding ring. Plans which 'integrated operations' in economic development were presented by cities as diverse as Birmingham and Oporto to the Fund administrators in Brussels for consideration. But they had to be supported by their governments.

Although cities and their regions can and do lobby over the heads of their governments, support will always be required from that source, a fact that needs to be remembered amidst much talk about 'Europe of the regions', suggesting that regions can almost go it alone. They cannot.

Cities in Britain and other parts of the European Union in any case are units which the European Commission finds it difficult to comprehend within a policy which is defined by regions. (Grants towards training and community development are handled by a different wing of the Commission which is less inhibited by the regional concept.) Cities in areas defined by the Commission as being in need, however, have benefited. Birmingham is a good example. It had received from European sources £260m in the ten years to 1994. The money must be matched by funds from local and national sources. Its major value is that it gives assurance of funding to an authority planning substantial developments that will be spread over several years, whereas finance from central government is allocated on an annual basis; it also saves the authority interest payments that would be incurred had it sourced the finance through borrowing. Debt charges had reached 17% of the Birmingham City Council budget before interest rates started to fall in 1992.

Pilot projects of aid have been targeted at deprived areas, even neighbourhoods, of cities which do not come within the European Commission's definition of need on their own account – London and Amsterdam, for instance. These are being extended into a special urban programme, designed to act as catalysts for urban initiatives.

The need to establish a deeper understanding of the special needs of cities will intensify as Europe moves to a more cohesive European Union. A study by the EU on the regional impact of proposals for monetary union predicted that areas not in the central core of Europe would be at a disadvantage without extra financial help to improve their competitive infrastructure, both physical and social. The European Union's Commissioner for Social Affairs told a conference that the social policies of the EU had failed 'in every city in Europe', and that the trickledown assumption underlying the emphasis on development had failed to tackle unemployment in marginalized communities.[22]

1.3 SMOOTHING THE EDGES OF RACE AND POVERTY

Cities have experienced huge changes in the composition of their populations over the last generation. American cities on their own (without the surrounding areas), often have a majority black population. These cities were built up initially on waves of immigration from different parts of Europe. They were followed by immigrants from central and south America, now from East Asia. English is a second language for 15% of people in the United States. Cities are not the only recipients of these invasions, but they tend to be the first stopping places. It is in cities that tensions mount between the newcomers from China, Korea, Vietnam, the existing Hispanic population and the indigenous black population. Some of the most feared gangs in Los Angeles and Miami are Chinese and Latinos.

In spring 1992, the worst racially based riots since the 1960s erupted in south Los Angeles, following the acquittal of four policemen suspected of beating up a black man. The riots had many roots, which included the economic sterility of young black men organized into gangs. They took vengeance on Asian shopkeepers. Atlanta witnessed some ugly incidents where the bitterness among young blacks erupted against whites. A black pastor in the city, however, predicted more recently that class, not race, would be more likely at the base of future tension, which would spring from the lack of low-skilled jobs for both blacks and whites.

The plight of the black ghettos in particular has been racking urban America. Between 1970 and 1990, 4 million whites departed from the big cities of America. So did middle-class blacks. The underclass was born in American speech in the 1970s. Mostly it was synonymous with poor blacks in ghettos. Chicago, now the scene of some of the most desperate inner-city problems of drugs, school drop-outs, murder and poor health, demonstrates what happened:

> Very quickly, around 1970, the ghettos went from being exclusively black to being exclusively black lower-class, and there was no countervailing force to the venerable, but always carefully contained, disorganized side of the ghetto culture.[23]

The ghettos and poverty and crime continue unabated. In 1992, Americans in poverty – defined as a measure of the real income needed to buy essential commodities – were 14.2% of the population, the highest since 1965, the year when President Johnson launched a huge federal anti-poverty programme which became known as the Great Society. In the big cities, figures from the 1990 Census showed that over 30% of the black population was in poverty, and around 15% of whites.

The debate rages between academics and politicians over how welfare might be reformed. The states make welfare payments. In most cases, welfare means 'aid to families with dependent children' (AFDC). Single people without children who do not get unemployment pay, just go without, hence the homeless who beg and sometimes just die on the streets. States want to reduce their welfare bills. Some have experimented with penalties to try and reduce the incidence of teenage pregnancies by cutting off AFDC when the mother becomes pregnant for the second time. One state will not issue driving licences to fathers of children who they do not support. Others have a more positive approach – endorsed in President Clinton's welfare reform proposals – of linking welfare to the provision of training opportunities and childcare facilities, to help single mothers into work.

But the social and racial tensions in cities are not confined to the poor. Canadian and European governments provide a safety net in terms of benefits for the poorest of their populations. Competition for jobs, accentuated by the loss of mostly well-paid blue-collar jobs in manufacturing, however, is being construed as caused by immigrants. 'Unlike in America, where the fundamental urban tension is that of race, the fundamental tension pulling at the social fabric of Europe's cities is that caused by long term unemployment'.[24]

In Frankfurt, for example, conditions of full employment virtually guaranteed high living standards for mainly white workers and their families. These jobs are increasingly difficult to find. Older immigrants, meanwhile, who were brought to the city by employers in the 1960s and 1970s when labour was in short supply, have frequently been paid off early and with too few pension years to enable them to enjoy the retirement they had anticipated. The situation in Germany is aggravated by the peculiar difficulties that many immigrants face in becoming citizens of the Republic.

The Netherlands does not have such constitutional restrictions on citizenship. But race is an issue in the poorer suburbs of Rotterdam which extreme right-wing political parties are quick to exploit. The social difficulties among immigrants to the Netherlands and Britain more often concern clashes between the first and second generations in immigrant families than the vengeant warfare of Los Angeles. To portray all ethnic minorities as indolent, living on benefits, as do some Dutch, is to ignore the fact that many have integrated into the economy, if not into society. One big employer in Rotterdam who trains new Dutch said that many of the young people dread being sent back to the 'home' villages in Turkey or North Africa for holidays. They want to be Dutch, and the authorities encourage this attitude.

So does Canada, frequently held up as the country which has most successfully adapted socially to the growing mix of races in its population. Toronto takes at least half of the immigrants into Ontario, about one-quarter of the total into Canada. From being a European and predominantly Anglo-Saxon city, Toronto has arrived at the point where at least one-quarter of its population has an ethnic minority background. Although particular districts in the city are associated traditionally with immigrant populations, there is nothing like the same concentration of poor minorities (including black, although these are hardly newcomers) as in the United States. There are certainly public housing blocks where drugs, crime, and other social problems are concentrated, but they are not yet places without hope. The spread of public housing and 'affordable' private rented accommodation to the suburbs has been responsible in part for this mix. Some of Canada's immigrants, into Toronto and Vancouver, the cities favoured by the Hong Kong Chinese, have brought substantial wealth to the commercial and residential areas of the city.

However, many immigrants and native Torontonians, living on benefits and dependent on low income work, must live in expensive private rented property. Spreading immigrants and poorer people around the city is increasingly hampered by the strong resistance of residents to the construction of affordable housing in their districts, particularly in the fast-growing suburbs. Meanwhile, the financial squeezes imposed on the city by the provincial and Federal governments are in stark contrast to the generous support that Toronto traditionally enjoyed. Spending on education, training and social programmes is not keeping pace with needs which have been accentuated by the changing economic structure in and around the city. Some fear that it is being pushed away from its European ethos towards the more socially and ethnically polarized American city and suburbs.

Immigration into Britain has been substantially curtailed in the last decade. Nearly a quarter of the population in some British cities and towns nevertheless has an ethnic minority background, dating from the 35 years following World War II when national policy was more welcoming of migrants from the West Indies, India, Pakistan and Bangladesh. London and Leicester in the East Midlands have the highest concentration, followed by Birmingham, Bradford, Slough and Smethwick, this last being a district adjacent to Birmingham. Migrants came mostly to a few districts, some the scene of race riots which erupted in Liverpool, Birmingham, London and Bristol in the early 1980s. They have not been repeated. More sensitive policing of immigrant areas has been a big factor. The most serious disturbances since then were in a poor white part of Newcastle during 1992. Drug-related crime in London and Manchester in particular, however, is on the increase. In 1993, 10 murders in Britain were officially attributed to crack cocaine, but the police worry that the drug which has wrecked the social fabric in neighbourhoods of many American cities is increasingly available and that violent crime will rise.

1.4 THE POWER OF THE COMMUNITY

In the morass of problems that are concentrated in cities, the word 'community' appears over and over again as the only solution. 'Fellowship' is one definition in *The Oxford Dictionary*, which is certainly not experienced only among the poor in cities. Yet community seems to have been something that people enjoyed in the poor districts before the razing of tight streets of houses and their replacement by municipal housing blocks separated by green space which rapidly became an unkempt no-man's land. The same housing blocks today are secure fortresses against the outside world. Rebuilding the old sense of fellowship, however, proved more intractable.

Even in the worst inner city areas, however, examples can be found where, according to Senator Bill Bradley,

> Heroic families do overcome the odds, where local neighbourhood leaders have turned around a local school, organized a health clinic, rehabilitated blocks of housing, where they have created 'islands of courage'.[25]

Community organizations can grow into sophisticated corporations which promote economic development in the neighbourhood, and are concerned with education, training and housing. Community development corporations in the United States have flourished, totalling between 2000 and 3000 across the country although there has been no national programme as such to encourage them. Community organizations often are much more modest. It might be, for example, an informal club in a Toronto suburb which helps to give immigrants and their families some reassurance in their adopted country, or, as in Birmingham, a group of women on a public housing estate who formed Safer Estates for Women to campaign and present their ideas on personal security to officialdom. Both groups are supported by a mix of charitable donations and local government.

'The best way to deflect people from a sense of alienation towards their cities and from a sense of anxiety about their future is for them to feel able to influence what happens.'[26] Urban policy in Britain attempts to address the need for community development. But at a policy level, the approach of Rotterdam Council with its 'Social Innovation' programme offers a significant pointer. The basic themes are self-help and community participation, encouraging poorer citizens to opt in rather than out of society and the economy while trying to induce a shift in popular thinking away from a simple assertion of rights towards an acceptance of responsibilities. The Atlanta Project's efforts to pick and sustain community leadership and development with the top-down help of business and voluntary contributions will be watched carefully to see if the two sides can work effectively.

1.5 WILL THE JOBS COME BACK?

Economic forecasters in 1994 were more optimistic about growth prospects than at any time in the last five years. They expected benefits arising out of the implementation of the Uruguay Round of the General Agreement on Tariffs and Trade, and recovery in the economies of the developed countries, with the possible exception of Japan. They noted that economies of the developing world, meanwhile, were not affected by the recession that hit the West. Unemployment in the 25 countries of the Organisation of Economic Development and Co-operation was expected to peak in 1994, at a record 35 million, representing 8.5% of the working population, falling to 8.3% in 1995.

Since 1990, the total number out of work in these countries had gone up by a staggering 10 million.[27] Unemployment in Europe is higher than the average for the OECD – 1994: 11.7% – reflecting the prolonged adjustment of high-cost industry sectors to the competition in the world economy. Although employment was forecast to nudge up slowly in parts of Europe, continued restructuring of strategic industries, like the automotive sector, would keep the overall rate high.

New employment has been concentrated in small companies and in the growth of work done under short-term contracts. Thirty per cent of all jobs in the European Union are from self-employment or in micro enterprises with less than 10 workers; small firms with less than 100 workers provide 55% of employment.[28] None of this is a concern in itself, except that small firms in Britain at least have been found to be more reluctant than larger companies to train workers in fear that they will be poached by other employers. Further, they are often loathe to take graduates into management. In cities, small firms are even more significant in the total workforce scene. In the Toronto area, 94% of all businesses employed less than 50 in 1991.

Self-employment and part-time work are equally important on the employment scene. In Birmingham, for example, the number of people involved went up by nearly 40% between 1981 and 1991. Economic development policies at national and city levels on both sides of the Atlantic are directed increasingly at encouraging business start-ups and the expansion of small and medium-sized businesses. In the United States, entrepreneurship is a significant means of entry to the economy for professional and less skilled ethnic minorities, or of re-entry after a spell in the corporate sector. The number of black-owned businesses grew by nearly 38% between 1982 and 1987, Hispanic-owned firms by 80%, and Asian by nearly 90%.[29]

The other major force in mopping up unemployment on both sides of the Atlantic has been the growth in part-time work. Politicians have actively encouraged it for this reason, and because it has helped to break down working practices characterized as 'inflexible'. Many people, particularly women with children, want to work part-time. But as presently construed by most employers, it tends to offer little in the way of job security, promotion prospects, training or pay.

1.6 SELF-HELP

The chapter started looking at some of the opportunities for business in cities which the new international economic order offers. But threats, of course, are implied as well. It is tougher for present-day cities than for the mayor of SimCity2000. There is no luxury of planning cities from scratch. The planners are stuck with outdated infrastructure; the social service departments face growing demands from the old, and from families without a member in work; and the finance department is frightened to suggest a rise in the property tax for fear of driving more business and residents out of the city.

Today's mayors and leaders are more likely to be university teachers, lawyers, and trade union officials, than the businessmen who went into politics in nineteenth-century England. They are not instinctively attuned to the latest twist in the international economy which could lead to one more factory closure in a district of their city that can scarce make up for the loss. Their re-election will depend not so much on their inspiration in helping to solve unemployment – which requires solutions over the longer term – but on how local taxpayers judge them on the basic services that they provide. Politicians at the higher levels of government have pushed for better management in local government, but frequently have not provided the support on which depend lasting improvements.

The more successful city governments will be those which, within all of the these limitations, can respond to the needs of each of their communities, be they employers, the elderly, the young, the high income earners, and the unemployed, and at those points where most, if not all, come together. Some city authorities have been more innovative than anyone would have dared to predict. Change has come out of desperate circumstance. Thus, Pittsburgh has transformed itself into a city of corporate headquarters; Baltimore buoyed up its centre on the back of the developed waterfront; and Cleveland's business community helped to take the declining city in hand. Over in Europe, Glasgow, not so long ago a byword for a place to avoid, has turned itself into a tourist attraction. Frankfurt spent heavily on culture as a means to being taken seriously by the international community. Lille, the capital of one of the hardest hit industrial regions in Europe, is launching itself as a city of the twenty-first century at the intersection of Europe's growing high-speed rail network. The list can go on.

Immediately, each success must be qualified when measured against the yardstick of: who has benefited? Redundant steelworkers did not find work in the offices, hotels and shopping centres built on the old steelworks site. The poor in Chicago gained little or nothing from the burst of investment in office towers and shopping malls in the 1980s. Meanwhile, in the poorer districts of cities, the economic cycle of recession and recovery has relatively little impact since a significant proportion of residents does not work at any time, at least not in the official labour market. Schemes which target job creation and training on disadvantaged sections of the population can have disappointing outcomes. Unemployment in Rotterdam is continuing upwards; similarly, in an area of Birmingham which benefited from extra resources to target training, the impact has been tiny not because the scheme itself did not work, but because there were so few new jobs for which people could be trained.

The successes also have to be seen in the context of disadvantage which is intensifying as it is handed on from one generation to the next. Crime, although not by any means unique to big urban areas, constitutes very real obstacles to the proper education of children who have one, or both, parents in prison. American inner city schools are the target of a host of government-funded and voluntary schemes which aim to alleviate the social difficulties of so many of the children. The school is developing as a sanctuary in some threatened neighbourhoods, in American and European cities, where children can stay after school hours rather than roam the streets. Imaginative study schemes to engage children's attention have been devised. But teaching staff in these inner city schools have a high level of sickness and absenteeism. The continuity in staff needed to give confidence to children is missing. In countries where government permits a certain amount of latitude to local authorities in spending between sectors, education has been downgraded in favour of, for example, property-based projects which are a more visual evidence of achievement. The cost of neglecting education will not show up quickly.

But basic educational skills are needed even for the most routine of jobs. 'America's economy has one and a half times more janitors than investment bankers, stockbrokers, lawyers, accountants and computer programmers put together.' But the new jobs will demand higher skills.

> Between 1992–2000, nine tenths of all new jobs need post secondary levels literacy and maths but only half of the new entrants into the workforce will have these levels . . . (with) Nearly half of the new jobs to come from managerial, professional and technical occupations.[30]

In 'globalizing' to meet the needs of the consumer, and so stay in business, companies locate where they believe they can optimize their competitive advantage. The opportunity to recruit the right labour force and to operate on a competitive cost basis is the top priority. The vocational skills base will become more important to manufacturers competing more and more in making high value products and possibly facing skilled labour shortages in Europe. Service employers expect new recruits to be able to work with technology. A good education structure is unlikely to make up the mind of the company on its own, but it can sway the company in favour of a particular location. Higher academic institutions with a record of working with business in the area will appeal to certain companies. And a city that can sustain a reputation for being safe and free of racial tensions will also be a factor. Porter advises companies to:

> find the localities whose regulations foreshadow those elsewhere. Some regions and cities will typically lead others in terms of their concern with social problems, such as safety, environmental quality, and the like. Instead of avoiding such areas, as some companies do, they should be sought out. The firm should define its internal goals as meeting or exceeding their standards. An advantage will result as other regions, and ultimately, other nations, modify regulations to follow suit.[31]

The cities which have sought their own solutions are most likely to hold their own. The critical areas to examine are the level of skills and educational attainment of the population, the degree of political and administrative co-operation with authorities in the surrounding areas and, finally, the achievement of common cause between business, politicians, residents and the voluntary (not-for-profit) agencies.

NOTES

1. *Sunday Times*, 6 March 1994.
2. Ohmae, K. (1990) *The Borderless World*, HarperCollins.
3. Jacobs, J. (1970) *The Economy of Cities*. Vintage Books.
4. Porter, M. (1990) *The Competitive Advantage of Nations*, Macmillan.
5. Ohmae, *The Borderless World, op. cit.*
6. Harvey, D. (1989) *The Urban Experience*, Blackwell.
7. King, A. (1990) *Global Cities*, Routledge.
8. Friedmann, J. (1986) *The World City Hypothesis: Development and Change*, quoted in King, *Global Cities, op. cit.*
9. Don Stevenson, Canadian Urban Institute, in interview with the author, February 1994.
10. Porter, *The Competitive Advantage of Nations, op. cit.*
11. Reich, R. (1992) *The Work of Nations*, Vintage Books.
12. Roger Taylor, Chief Executive, Birmingham City Council, in interview with the author, May 1994.
13. Friedman, J. and Miller, J. (1968) The urban field. *Journal of the American Institute of Planners*, **31**. Quoted in Nelson, A. (1990) Regional patterns of exurban industrialisation: results of a preliminary investigation. *Economic Development Quarterly* **4**(4).
14. Fothergill, S., Kitson, M. and Monk, S. (1985) *Urban industrial change: the causes of the urban–rural contrast in manufacturing employment trends*, HMSO.

15. Leinberger, C. and Lockwood, C. (1986) How business is reshaping America, *Atlantic Monthly*, **258**(4), October.
16. Garreau, J. (1991) *Edge City: Life on the Frontier*, Doubleday Books.
17. Persky, J., Sclar, E. and Wiewel, W. (1991) *Does America Need Cities?* Economic Policy Institute, Washington DC.
18. Gilbert, R. (1994) *Holding the Centre: Downtown Toronto and the Toronto Region*, Canadian Urban Institute.
19. Osborne, D. and Gaebler, T. (1992) *Re-inventing Government*, Addison-Wesley Publishing Co.
20. Kreukels, A. M. J. and Salet, W. G. M. (eds) (1992) *Debating Institutions and Cities*. Netherlands Scientific Council for Government Policy.
21. Treaty of Rome, 1957.
22. *Irish Times*, 19 October 1993.
23. Lemann, N. (1986) The origins of the underclass, *Atlantic Monthly*, **258**(1), July.
24. *The Economist*, 30 July 1994.
25. Speech on the Senate floor, 26 March 1924; edited version *Philadelphia Inquirer*, 5 April 1992.
26. McConnell, C. (1993) *Trickle Down or Bubble Up?* Report of OECD/CDF Conference.
27. OECD (1994) *Employment Outlook*, OECD.
28. Centre for Small and Medium Sized Enterprises (1993) *Annual Report*, Warwick University.
29. Black entrepeneurship, *Wall Street Journal*, April 1992.
30. Carnevale, A. (1994) American Society for Training and Development, *The Economist*, 15 January 1994.
31. Porter, *The Competitive Advantage of Nations, op. cit.*

Atlanta

2

Figure 2.1 Atlanta, Georgia, in the south-eastern United States.

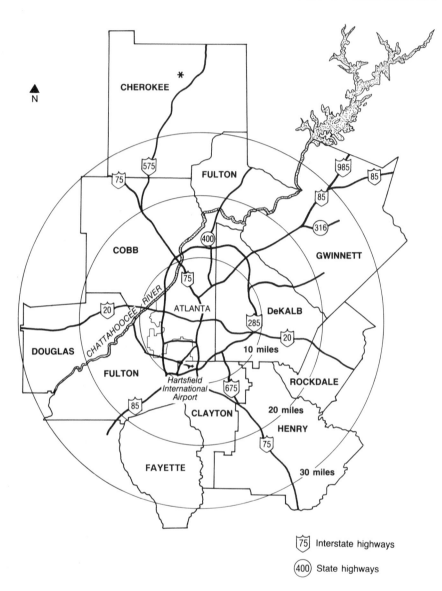

Figure 2.2 The ten counties of the Atlanta region. (* added in 1993)

Table 2.1 Basic facts about Atlanta

(a) Population

City of Atlanta	Atlanta region[1]	Metropolitan Atlanta[2]
415 200	2 466 800	2.9m

Notes:
1. 9 counties region.
2. 20 counties Metropolitan Statistical Area.
Source: Census, 1990, adjusted.

(b) Median household income, Atlanta region, 1990 = $36 742

(c) Ethnic minorities (i.e. black and other races), 1992

Region	Percentage of population
City of Atlanta	69.3
Atlanta region	31.4

Note: non-hispanic blacks total 86% of the minority population.

(d) Employment by sector, Atlanta region, 1980–1992

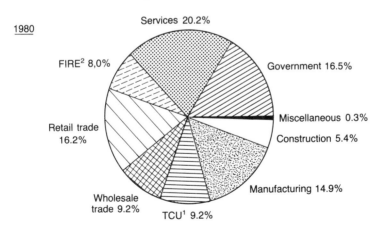

Industry share of employment (%)

1980

Services 20.2%

FIRE[2] 8,0%

Government 16.5%

Miscellaneous 0.3%

Construction 5.4%

Retail trade
16.2%

Manufacturing 14.9%

Wholesale
trade 9.2%   TCU[1] 9.2%

[1] TCU – see overleaf
[2] FIRE – see overleaf

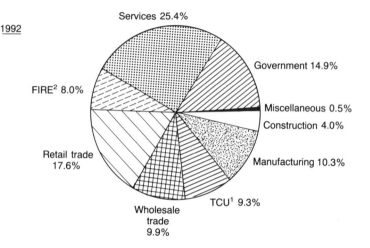

Notes:
1. Transportation, communication and utilities.
2. Finance, insurance and real estate.

Source: Atlanta Regional Commission.

(e) Top five corporations (by employment), Atlanta region

　　1. American Telephone & Telegraph
　　2. Delta Airlines
　　3. Lockheed Aeronautical Systems
　　4. Southern Bell Telephone & Telegraph
　　5. Georgia Power

2.1 INTRODUCTION

Pride in a progressive city

The greatest advocates for Atlanta are its own citizens. No matter if they are from New York, Chicago, St Paul, from Nigeria, Mexico, or from Georgia itself, black or white, few people have a bad word to say about the city, not, at least, to an obvious visitor. 'It's a good city', 'It's a great city', 'You can get on here.' Maynard Jackson, three-times mayor of the City of Atlanta (until 1993) used to say: 'It's not a perfect city, but it's one of the best.' It's the American Dream of a place where a good living might be earned, wherever you started from, of getting your kids educated through college, of owning your own home, of retiring in good health, where it is warm all year round.

The basis for this confidence in Atlanta was almost uninterrupted economic growth between the late 1970s and 1990, followed by recession, but already recovering by 1993. Inward investment is one source of growth – over 1,500 companies located in the Atlanta region between 1983 and 1992, 362 of them described by the Chamber of Commerce as 'international'. When Atlanta's civic and business leaders go out to sell Atlanta round the world, they can boast that *Fortune* magazine frequently ranks it in the top ten business cities in the United States. *Fortune* put it in the category of relatively new business centres along with Houston, and Raleigh/Durham, which 'supplant provincialism with savoir-faire to attract global companies'.[1]

Metropolitan Atlanta (20 counties, defined by the US Census Bureau) has pulled in a host of foreign affiliates in the last 25 years, in manufacturing, business services, hotel groups, airlines, from every part of the globe, many of them big names. Atlanta can meet most of the varied demands which international companies expect of a city: international airport and highways system which make it the communications capital of the south-eastern United States, with its population of 40 million, high quality business accommodation and housing, advanced telecommunications, core of business services, research institutions.

Some recent corporate arrivals include British Telecom which set its international subsidiary, Syncordia, in the Atlanta area, while Holiday Inn International and United Parcel Services were two of the corporations which have picked Atlanta in the last few years for their head offices. Add these relocation coups to home-grown corporations like Coca-Cola and CNN (Cable News Network, part of the Turner broadcasting group), mix in medical research institutions – the US Centres for Disease Control, the American Cancer Society – and not-for-profit (charities) headquarters, and Atlanta can seem a heady cocktail.

At the core of Atlanta's growth is its ability to create jobs and thereby to attract people. Every year they come, skilled workers, professionals, top medical researchers, and the more ordinary in search of the opportunity to better themselves. Many are black 'homing pigeons' coming back south in the belief that they have better prospects in Atlanta than in the Northern cities. Even in the 1990–91 recession, the nine counties Atlanta Region (as defined for the Atlanta Regional Commission) added between 30 000 and 40 000 residents a year. Between 1992 and 1996, the average annual increase will have been in the order of 63,600[2]. Atlanta's growth has been remarkable even by the standards of the sunbelt southern states. Net in-migration over the last 20 years totalled over 600 000 people. New jobs run parallel with the influx of people, hence the attraction of the area. The region's job count is more than 3.5 times that of 1960. Some 70 500 new jobs a year were forecast for the period 1992–96.[3]

The heady figures should not obscure some more worrying aspects of the Atlanta story. Crime, drugs, homelessness, unemployment, the four most visible signs of urban decline, have hardly been addressed. Public education standards are poor, not only in the city proper but also in many suburban districts. Atlanta's economic success to a considerable degree is dependent on its being able to attract trained people from other parts of the country and overseas. As far as the first category goes, there are signs of greater reluctance to uproot and move long distances.

The successful side of Atlanta owes much to the band of business and civic leaders – sometimes they were one and the same – who succeeded each other over the generations to make politics work for the benefit of business, and, by extension, for part of the community. Atlanta was not a city dominated by any one political party, but by a business elite which wielded considerable influence in the way that the city developed. These leaders lobbied and got money from state and Federal governments to invest in expressways, the airport, rapid transit, in preparation for new business, rather than the more normal pattern where communications followed population and business. But Atlanta in the 1980s could not have happened without the black leadership of the 1960s which grew out of its educated, black middle class. It produced leaders, most notably Martin Luther King, who were to usher in the mostly peaceful desegregation of the city.

From railroad terminus to the world's sixth largest airport

Atlantans point out that their city was never based on a plantation economy. It began humbly as the site for the terminus of the Western & Atlantic Railroad. Twenty years later, at the outbreak of the Civil War, four railroads converged on the area, and Atlanta was already a centre of manufacturing and distribution. The city's charter dates back to 1847, when the population was 2000. Several pioneer Atlantans petitioned to have their home named as the state capital. They succeeded in March 1868. Four months later, the city was re-admitted to the Union. Atlanta was already launched on its campaign to become the capital of the south. In 1895, the city staged the International Exposition, one of a series of international fairs held across the United States between 1876 and 1916. In 1926, leading members of the Chamber of Commerce formed the Forward Atlanta Commission – which is still the promotion body for metropolitan Atlanta – and soon embarked on a sales campaign. The slogan was that 'What New York is to the East, Chicago to the West, San Francisco to the Pacific, Atlanta is to the South'. Companies which came to the area included National Biscuit (Nabisco), Southern Railway, and Sears Roebuck (of Chicago) which put its south-eastern headquarters into a vast building close to the centre which did not finally close its doors until the early 1990s.

Up to the late 1960s, the politics and business of the city were pretty much intertwined. The mayors of the City of Atlanta relied on the support of the business community for their election. Atlanta then was a predominantly white city but these politicians, some strict segregationists, relied on a tacit support from the leaders of the black community. Atlanta did not experience the violence of other parts of the South during the civil rights period. The story of how the mayor ordered that the funeral of the assassinated Martin Luther King take place in his home town at the expense of the business community was an example of how a few key figures, white and black, had their fingers on the pulse of the city at a critical time. 'Nobody paid for any food for four days', recalled a participant. It might seem of little importance in the light of the solemnity of the occasion. But Atlanta did not erupt.

And so the city won federal funds. In 1962, the airport had been renamed Hartsfield International although its only international flight was to Mexico. Money came in for urban renewal, the expansion of the airport, highways and public transport. By the 1980s, Hartsfield was the second largest airport in the world in terms of air traffic movements. William Hartsfield, who was mayor during and after World War II, has been cast in Atlanta's folk history as one of the 'visionary leaders' whose name, along with Ivan Allen Jr who was mayor in the 1960s, still trips off the tongues of Atlantans seeking reasons for the city's success.

Atlanta enjoyed a degree of common purpose while it was struggling to make its mark on the nation. But maturing in the global economy makes rigorous demands on the skills of corporate leaders. Business and government has grown much more fragmented geographically and ideologically and the business leadership is less obviously identifiable.

And Atlanta is not the only jewel in the region's crown. Tampa and Orlando in Florida were muscling in during the 1980s. Dallas is an arch-rival for international and national investment. Control of Atlanta's two biggest banks passed in the last few years to banks headquartered in Charlotte, North Carolina. The collapse of Eastern Airlines in 1991 was reflected in reduced passenger movements at Hartsfield, and, although new, smaller airlines have started up at the airport, the seemingly impregnable advantage that Atlanta had created in Hartsfield as an airport hub for the region had itself proved vulnerable.

Atlanta has strengths in a fairly diverse economy. The 1990–91 recession, when some 26 000 jobs were lost in one year, had bottomed out by 1993. By 1992–93, using job creation as the yardstick, the economy was picking up rapidly, and acting as a catalyst for growth in the state of Georgia. Many of the new jobs, however, were temporary, part-time and low-paid.[4]

Questions confronting the city

Atlanta must hold its lead position as communications hub in the southeast. It must capitalize on the presence of companies in telecommunications, media and entertainment to establish a national lead in multimedia. And it has to deal much more satisfactorily than it has done so far with poverty and unemployment in the city. The issue is enormous. Human services and more efficient government, and development which is sustainable with the environment, will depend on some sort of accommodation reached between government and special boards in the region.

Atlanta is more diverse, more complex, than it was in the 1960s and 1970s. It must resolve some of its problems more definitively than to date if it is to confound its critics that it is 'all gloss and little substance'. 'Atlanta was built on "puffery" ', admits a businessman who was actively involved in the heady days of the late 1960s, 'but periodiocally, it would emotionally galvanize itself into doing things.'[5] The campaign which captured the Olympics for the city in 1996 was one such time, and demonstrated the sort of partnership for which Atlanta was renowned. The Olympics presents one big opportunity to make a greener and more attractive city; the Atlanta Project, set up by former President Jimmy Carter in 1991 to tackle the city's Third World type poverty, presents a different sort of opportunity. Both projects had in common that the private sector provides the bulk of the funds, although they both need support from the public sector. Partnership in the 1990s calls for finer skills perhaps than those that worked in the past. These projects will be a test of whether present-day Atlanta can get them together.

2.2 THE CHANGING FACE OF ATLANTA

A highway to everyone's door

Atlanta in the 1990s is a loose amalgam of suburbs, which are towns in their own right. The developers' tentacles stretch ever further into the countryside. The map of the area (p. 42) shows the web of highways crossing the region and the perimeter route. Further out, good cross routes are less in evidence. The outer ring highway which would have been over 30 miles from the centre seemed unlikely to go ahead, except for one section. Only one new highway link, I-675, was added in the 1980s, although many freeways were expanded, and in 1993, the Georgia 400 extension was opened, to speed access between Perimeter Centre, one of the growth centres due north of the city, through Buckhead, to downtown.

A new state highway had also been finally given the go-ahead on the eastside of Atlanta. The need for the highway had been widely questioned. In the early 1980s, the case for it was made by being linked to the provision of an access road to the Carter presidential library and policy centre which was backed by the then mayor of the city of Atlanta, Andrew Young, despite fierce, organized neighbourhood opposition. The go-ahead was disappointing for planners who had hoped to demonstrate that Atlanta could move to a more public transport-oriented mode following federal legislation in 1991 aimed at encouraging public transport as an alternative to the automobile and its demand that more highways be built. The overriding of community opposition, however, was unfortunately in line with Atlanta's past programmes of clearances in preparation for alternative use.

A city moving to the suburbs

The highway network is the most important location factor in Atlanta. Growth points are predominantly on the northern side of the city, although the airport in the south of Fulton County is a major exception to the northern drift. Atlanta was one of the cities picked to highlight the changes in the patterns of development in the urban areas from the early 1980s, illustrating in particular this growth of settlements based on highway intersections.[6] The authors christened them 'urban villages', picking out Perimeter Center and Cumberland/Galleria as examples and which are now two of the fastest growing centres in the region. Far from being isolated clusters of office blocks, these new office centres were beginning to create their own spheres of economic influence, they argued, spawning apartment blocks, hotels, shopping centres and leisure facilities. The influence of the core city was diminishing, to become just one of a series of linked urban satellites across a region in place of the traditional central city surrounded by suburbs.

> Few cities have been transformed by the urban-village phenomenon as rapidly as Atlanta . . . In 1980 downtown Atlanta was the metropolitan region's unchallenged centre for all kinds of office employment. Although urban-village cores were emerging around shopping malls at the intersections of major highways, office space was limited . . . By 1985 – just five years later – this pecking order had changed completely . . . [Downtown Atlanta was] losing its metropolitan hegemony and becoming just another one of the region's urban-village cores.[7]

The pace of growth was illustrated at Perimeter Center, at the intersection of I-285 and Georgia 400, which had gained 7.6m sq. ft of new office space in those five years, and Cumberland/Galleria at the intersection of I-285 and I-75 had put on 10.6m sq. ft. Downtown developments had

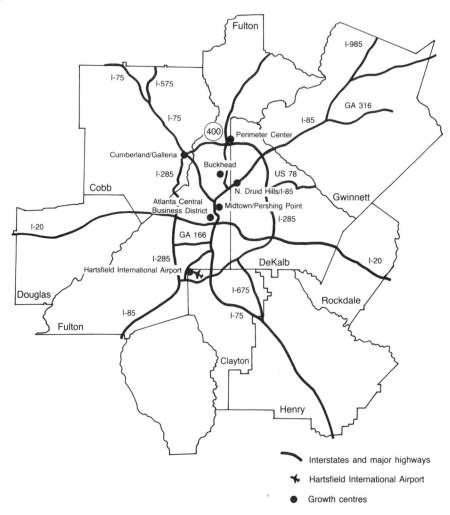

Figure 2.3 Growth centres of the Atlanta region. *Source:* Atlanta Regional Commission.

equalled 4.3m sq ft in the same period. They were by then sought after as head office locations, whereas in their early years, tenants had been mostly banking and insurance back offices.

The second half of the 1980s, however, was a time of partial recovery downtown, although only with the aid of tax concessions and grants. New office towers included that for Georgia-Pacific. The 'festival market' place, Underground Atlanta, was finally launched in 1989. The Georgia Dome sports centre opened in 1992, creating 1500 new jobs in what had been a marginal area of the city. The fragility of the central city economy can be seen from the fact that the Central Business District added 11 000 jobs during the 1980s, but then lost 4800 in the 1990–91 recession.

Away from the centre, but still within the city, the growth points are in Buckhead, in the north, which would shortly have a station on the Atlanta rapid transit system (known as MARTA); Midtown, just a mile or so north of the centre, which has been rapidly taking shape as the relocation out of the downtown business district and well served by the MARTA and two major highways; N. Druid Hills north-east of Midtown, on the I-85; and Hartsfield to the south.

One in three working people were reported in the 1990 Census as giving the city as their workplace. But most of the companies which set up in the Atlanta area from other parts of the United States go for suburban locations. So do overseas companies and American corporations which want regional offices in the area. Atlanta's home-grown high-tech companies, with the exception of the Ted Turner-founded CNN which is downtown, have also opted for the suburbs, mostly along the Georgia 400 corridor. The preference for the suburbs is influenced by all of the obvious factors, like site availability and space to expand, and rents and taxes lower than within the city boundaries, plus the detachment that the outer suburbs, at least, can enjoy away from the social problems that predominate in the older part of the region.

Atlanta's downtown is small and not at all distinguished, but it has so far avoided the near total desertion that happened in Detroit, for example, from the late 1960s on. Its future is uncertain. In European eyes, the current plans when effected will never transform the centre into something that can rival some of the older American cities, and it does not have a natural focal point. But the planned new line-up of central city functions outlined later will be watched with interest.

The Olympics – redemption for downtown Atlanta?

Atlanta's promoters see the selection of the city for the 1996 Centennial Olympic Games as the occasion which will say that it really has arrived on the international stage. The celebration will not only be Atlanta's, but much of the rest of Georgia breaking out of the suspicions of Southern backwardness that are still cast upon the state. Most of the events, however, will take place within a three-mile radius of the centre.

Atlanta's Olympics bid was spearheaded by the private sector, an important asset for the business promotion bodies like the Chamber of Commerce, in co-operation with the City Council. The organization is managed by the Atlanta Committee for the Olympic Games, which is chaired by Andrew Young, Atlanta's most famous black figure since Martin Luther King, and twice mayor of the city in the 1980s. The manager is a downtown lawyer who has played a prominent role in city affairs. The finance for the $209m Olympic Stadium, and the Olympics Village was scheduled to be raised from the private sector. One of the main sponsors of this and past Olympics is the Atlanta-based Coca-Cola Company.

Nobody in business believed that the 16-day event would make a significant impact on the economy, or even that it would provide a spur for the property sector, but it was viewed by the city planners as a heaven-sent chance to push ahead on environmental improvement plans that had been sitting on the shelf for so long. A relatively modest $38m programme was signalled to create a new park, and add greenery to the drab downtown streets and overground parking lots. The event was also coupled with the need to catch up on providing less visible improvements to the water distribution system and the network of sewers, and to strengthen bridges and viaducts. All of these needs had lagged behind while the new office blocks soared upwards. In Midtown, the shakiness of some of the infrastructure was horribly underlined when the car park of one new hotel literally caved in in 1993, causing two deaths, over a collapsed sink pipe.

Two years before the Games were due to take place, there were all the signs of brinkmanship between the providers of funds and those planning to spend the money. City Council president Marvin Arrington warned, 'The city's almost bankrupt, and I'd like to find out where we're going to get the money.'[8]

The mayor, Bill Campbell, was locked in conflict early in 1994 with the city's property taxpayers over how to fund maintenance of the bridges and viaducts. Capital improvements were costed at $149m, to be raised by an issue of bonds to which the electorate had to agree in the required referendum. Sanction for bond issues to pay for water and sewer improvements is a separate issue. An alternative proposal was that the county in which the city is situated should levy an additional 1% on the sales tax between 1994 and 1996, amounting to an increase in the tax of about 17%. Half of the proceeds would go to the city. Either measure would have to be approved in the State legislature.

Budget shortfall brings the City close to the brink

Atlanta must poll its taxpayers if it wants to raise money for capital projects. It does not happen very often. With 1996 looming up, some compromise between taxpayers and the mayor was anticipated. The City's current expenditure had meanwhile taken a plunge for the worse. Campbell's campaign in 1993 had centred on there being no need to raise taxes. One month after his inauguration, the budget shortfall was revealed as $34–36m. This shook the city. Atlanta had not teetered on bankruptcy. Now it was in danger of drifting into the sort of trap that had ensnared New York, Cleveland, Philadelphia and others at various times.

The City's general fund comes mainly from property taxpayers. The largest spending allocation, about one quarter, goes on police. Some 15% was scheduled for public works. The airport which is owned by the City normally produces an extra contribution to the City budget, and revenue is derived from charges for water and sewerage services. Social services are the responsibility of county government. City schools (but not suburban) are run by an independent, elected Board of Education, for which finance is raised separately.

The City must maintain a sufficiently large tax base to finance essential services but not deter the business and household taxpayers or tourists, who pay a bed tax. Some 20–25% of office space built in the latter part of the 1980s was still unoccupied in the 1990s.

2.3 ATLANTA'S SOCIAL CIRCUMSTANCES

The inner city ingredients of poverty and crime

The City of Atlanta population is nearly 70% black, which is by far the highest concentration of minorities anywhere in the region. The enforced movement of people during the upheavals of urban renewal was followed by the exodus of most of the remaining white population prior to desegregation in the schools in the city, and the split was reversed. The City also has the highest incidence of poverty as defined by the Federal government, which takes into account not only household income, but also the number of persons in the household and their ages.

Being black does not necessarily mean being poor. But 61% of the population in poverty in the nine-counties region is black. And poverty is heavily concentrated in and around the city. Crime and drugs cast fear over a wide area. One estimate puts drugs and other illegal activities as equal to about 10% of the city's economy. Even the downtown has streets which need to be avoided. But the people who really suffer are those living in neighbourhoods which are in the control of drug barons.

> Like most cities, Atlanta tries to accentuate the positive: its championship sports teams, its rapid-transit system, its symphony orchestra, the towering additions to its skyline. But conditions have deteriorated to the point where some people have given up hope of ever having the things most Americans take for granted: a decent home, a safe community, adequate health care, an education, a living wage.[9]

Crime and poverty are not the province of the older city areas and housing projects alone. Ten thousand respondents to a survey organized by the Atlanta Regional Commission named 'crime and drugs' as the number one issue that Atlanta must address.[10] Atlanta is consistently in one league which it does not boast about. As well as being in the Fortune top ten business cities, it is also in the top ten cities measured by the violent crime rate per head of population.

The Atlanta Project

Poverty, homelessness and drug addiction in his own back yard moved former president, Jimmy Carter, to set up an ambitious programme, The Atlanta Project (TAP) in 1991 to address poverty in Atlanta. Carter's relations with the Atlanta business community during his years as Governor of Georgia had never been warm. But it was to those same downtown businesses that he turned for support to get TAP under way. It was a gamble. Atlanta business was comfortable enough with philanthropic foundations. The Woodruff Foundation, set up by the Coca-Cola family, is an outstanding example of support for projects and research. But TAP was planned on a specifically anti-poverty drive. It was ambitious enough to attract attention across the United States, in two respects: the extent of the territory that it was to cover, by classifying 20 districts roughly equivalent to the catchment area of a high school into 'clusters', covering most of the city and spilling over into adjacent neighbourhoods, with a total target area housing about half a million people; and it aimed to build up a responsible core of leaders in each cluster which would carry on the anti-poverty programme when TAP wound itself up.

Twenty-seven major companies, 21 universities and colleges, agreed to help. The realization was growing that the conditions in which part of the Atlanta population lived were intolerable for a city selling itself as one of the most progressive business centres in the country. For at least five years, which is the anticipated lifespan of TAP, they pledged $15m in cash and $13m in kind. Some of the money and expertise was to be channelled through project offices set up in the clusters, some was scheduled to go into existing programmes already sponsored by the private sector, like the Metro Literacy Network, and the programmes run by the City council. The council had staged a forum to plan action against poverty in 1992. But it decided to co-operate with TAP, even if some members were slightly suspect about the inevitable 'parachuting-in' nature of a short-term project, and also provided office space for TAP.

The idea was to get at least one corporate sponsor in each cluster. By 1994, only two were still without a corporate partner. The nature of the business support is not uniform. Companies release staff to train the co-ordinators appointed by TAP to run each cluster, helping them to learn the basics of strategic planning, and to verse them in management and accounting disciplines. The role of the CEOs of the supporting corpora-

Figure 2.4 Ex-President and Mrs Jimmy Carter have put their weight behind The Atlanta Project, ensuring huge publicity for a regeneration effort. *Courtesy of Tom England.*

tions is not passive. They are expected to attend a short meeting each month at TAP's Centre.

One of TAP's early successes was to get thousands of volunteers, who included a sprinkling of CEOs, to take part in a short campaign encouraging parents to take pre-school-age children to centres where they would be immunized against childhood diseases. Despite such immunization being covered by federal support, many parents had still neglected to take up the opportunity to eradicate early childhood diseases.

TAP's efforts were watched closely by community workers across the United States. It afforded an insight into the complex problems of creating community where none existed. Carter had picked Dan Sweat, director of the downtown Central Atlanta Progress (CAP) group of big corporations from 1973 to 1988, to direct TAP. He had been a key player in negotiating deals between downtown business and civic leaders during that time. He was the right person to solicit the support of CEOs for Carter's project since they knew and trusted him, while Carter was an outsider. Sweat pulled in other long-standing contacts from politics, the voluntary sector and education and asked them to muster support from their networks of contacts.

The fundamental idea behind TAP was that it would help poor people to help themselves. If it did not do that, then it would have been little better than a charitable campaign. In principle, it sounded simple. It actually proved much harder than the founders had expected.

The easy bits were doing what the organizers were experienced in doing. A lobby to persuade the State legislature to allow a $2000 tax credit to employers who created jobs in the poorest counties in Georgia was a success, for instance. The biggest difficulties came in organizing the clusters, and identifying prospective co-ordinators who could hold the trust of the community. Rivalries between competing groups quickly surfaced. In some neighbourhoods, nobody came forward at all. Eighteen months after it was set up, it was clear that, instead of building up communities, TAP was drifting, despite the groundswell of goodwill.

Sweat admitted that his model had been his old employer, CAP, which worked according to a strictly top-down approach to getting things done. CAP had a small staff, used top consultants when needed, formed special task forces to address particular issues, would burn the midnight oil until they had got a plan together. 'I was that kind of animal. I have been a gunner. For me, this way was natural.'[11] But it did not suit everybody. CAP could set its own internal goals, and measure itself accordingly. But TAP was wide open to being judged by everybody according to its objectives, which, according to one insider, had demonstrated the 'lack of early conceptualisation in the programme'.

TAP's director, overwhelmed by dozens of people daily beating a path to his door, was asked by Carter if he wanted a deputy. He replied: 'No, I want a top-flight African-American, on the payroll, to report to me, but to be very independent.'[12] He picked Jane Smith who had been development director of the Martin Luther King Centre for Nonviolent Social Change, and she took over the management. Sweat concentrated on the direction and publicizing the progress of TAP across the country.

2.4 EDUCATION – INVESTING IN A FUTURE WORKFORCE

'We continue to have a sufficiently skilled work force because of immigration, and thus are surviving in spite of the schools.'[13] Atlanta has a better educated and a younger population than the median for the nation, thanks to immigration. But there could be no complacency about the state of public education in the Atlanta area. Georgia state, which is

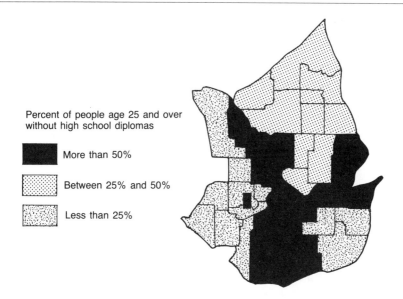

Percent of people age 25 and over without high school diplomas

■ More than 50%

▨ Between 25% and 50%

▨ Less than 25%

Figure 2.5 The share of the City of Atlanta without high-school diplomas, 1990. *Source*: Atlanta Regional Commission.

responsible for education outside the City, 'simply cannot deliver by itself. Many issues facing public education originate outside of schools.'[14]

The business and politics of education

Atlanta business, through the Chamber of Commerce, picked up on the politics of education in 1993. A slate of candidates to stand in elections to the Board of Education was put up. The City leaders had given tacit support to the idea. Candidates were carefully selected and vetted for their sympathies towards a business agenda in education. Their campaigns were paid for by business. With one exception, the candidates were all successful.

Pressure from business for changes in the system had been intensified when a top businessman, Kent C. Nelson, chairman and CEO, United Parcel Services, had made it known publicly that his company's choice to locate in Atlanta might have been different if the decision had been made on education alone. He later agreed to be vice chair of education at the Chamber. Odie C. Donald, president BellSouth Mobility, was picked to chair the Atlanta Partnership of Business and Education. Soon after the Chamber-nominated candidates took office, the superintendent of the School Board resigned. The Chamber offered to help in finding a replacement with the help of a recruitment agency, repeating a similar exercise when it helped the City fill the general manager aviation post at the airport.

'The business community stayed away from the school system, and a heavy cost was paid for that', said the Chamber's outgoing education chair – Guy W. Millner, chairman of Norrell Temporary Services. 'Today, it's just a different climate. It's not as adversarial. There's much more of a partnership.'[15]

Business and education in Atlanta were no strangers. In the past, the leaders had played their part at the state level which had 'helped the city peacefully desgregate(d) its public school system, contributing to an end of massive resistance in the South'.[16]

But inner-city schools in general in Atlanta have low achievement levels. The rating of achievement in the Scholastic Aptitude Test, and various other tests, showed that city schools, and some suburban schools, were frequently below the average for Georgia as a whole, which, in any case, falls below the national average. 'The most pressing areas of concern (in the metropolitan Atlanta area) are illiteracy, worker preparation, drop-out rates, student–teacher ratios and teacher preparedness.'[17] Drop-out rates from high schools in the city, had been put officially at 30% but were almost certainly higher in some areas. The picture was not uniform. 'Magnet' schools which were created to attract bright pupils from outside catchment areas by offering a curriculum that allows students to specialize in subjects like communications and engineering have had some success. Around half of the children in the city proper attend private and parochial schools.

The business community was concerned about standards, but also convinced that too high a proportion of education money was being swallowed up in administration. This is a problem that is being tackled in many cities. School Board bureaucrats had often proved resistant to any new ideas that precipitated changes in the classroom. Classes are large, teachers restricted in their teaching methods, and highly regulated by their terms and conditions.

New schemes to combat poor standards

Business and education partnerships had blossomed in Atlanta, in the sense that companies would link with a particular school. What they did with the partnership, however, varied from company to company. An investigation by the Chamber of Commerce found that some partnerships had more public relations than educational value in them.[18] Another scheme had counsellors going into classrooms to encourage students at risk to stay through school, and to go on to higher education. And another scheme guaranteed to make up any shortfall in finance that would prevent a student taking up a college place.

Figure 2.6 Kids at work: American business is worried by low levels of educational attainment. *Courtesy of Georgia Institute of Technology.*

Mentoring is another idea used in schools across the United States. Mentors might be retired church members or young, black men who have succeeded in sport or business, who can be particularly valuable in providing a role model for young black male children whose home circumstances put them in the high-risk category of falling into crime and dropping out of school. And social events have been staged in schools to encourage reluctant parents and guardians to bury their feelings that schools are alien places. One elementary school whose pupils come almost totally from Techwood Homes, the oldest public housing project in the United States, had been adopted in 1992 into the 'Learning Village' programme that was being set up in selected schools across the country. Its aim was to

embrace learners from childhood through adulthood, engage grandparents and other seniors to prepare infants and toddlers for accelerated progress, and involve parents in formal learning experiences with their children. The curriculum will stress self-knowledge and offer global perspectives . . .

This school got blue-chip backing to stimulate more innovative teaching over a three-year term. As well as claiming grant aid from the New American Schools Development Corporation, it is supported by Georgia Institute of Technology, the Coca-Cola Company, which has its head office in the vicinity of the school, and IBM, another big employer in Atlanta.

2.5 RACE AND CLASS

Atlanta claims boldly that it is 'a community proud of its ethnic diversity and harmony'.[19] Not everybody would agree. Atlanta is not the land of opportunity for black people which is so often depicted by its promoters. Bill Stanley, black partner in a professional firm and graduate of Georgia Institute of Technology, told a public seminar in downtown Atlanta organized by the Atlanta History Society in early 1994 that, despite his education and job status, he was 'still not welcome in some places in Atlanta'.

A dominating issue in annexation

The race issue has dominated the question of the city and its boundaries. Most of the City of Atlanta lies in Fulton County, whose population in 1992 was 685 800, making it the most populated county in the Atlanta Region's total population of 2 381 000, and part of DeKalb county. Fulton districts range from some of the wealthiest to some of the poorest in Atlanta. The ethnic minorities population (black and other races) stabilized between 1980 and 1992 at around 52–53%, but in DeKalb, it rose from 30 to 47% during this period. If the City wanted to annex part of the adjacent districts in these and other counties, a referendum in the area proposed for annexation would need to be held. A taste of suburban residents' determination to keep out anything to do with the City was provided in a poll in two counties – Gwinnett and Cobb – on a proposal by MARTA to extend the transit system out there. The result was a resounding defeat for the proposal, which was unashamedly based on race considerations. Rather than attempt to broaden the City's boundaries,

Table 2.2 Population by race, Atlanta region, 1900–92

Year	Total population	White		Black and other races	
		Number	Percent of total	Number	Percent of total
1900	249 555	162 764	65.2	86 791	34.8
1960	1 062 020	817 486	77.0	244 534	23.0
1992*	2 535 500	1 738 344	68.6	797 156	31.4

*Adjusted for 1990 census undercount.
Source: Atlanta Regional Commission.

some form of co-operation on services is now talked about with Fulton County, and possibly DeKalb, with a view to moderating property taxes.

White property taxpayers in Fulton County, meanwhile, resent the fact that part of their taxes is being used to support poor blacks in the city.

> Whites in this county are upset about many things . . . The white community's anger is directed at 'those people in the city' for whom we have 'done too much'. As the economy shrinks, the resentment by whites of public programmes for blacks increases,

said Michael Lomax, who, as chair of Fulton County Commission, was one of Atlanta's leading black politicians.

In Fulton County, he had earlier been confronted with an attempt by constituents to force a recall election, prompted by the possibility of a tax increase to finance new programmes to fight poverty. He made it clear that this was 'segregation' at work. One month before the Los Angeles riots took place in April 1992, he warned that

> this country is very close to where racial animosity can emerge into violence . . . A lot has changed in the South; a lot has not; the rural poor have become the urban poor. The changes for the educated have been dramatic. I can eat where I want. But for 30–40% of my people it has not changed . . . Atlanta is a city of tremendous hype, the reality is very different.[20]

Lomax later ran for mayor of the city of Atlanta. The campaign turned into a two-horse race between himself and Campbell, who was backed by the incumbent, Maynard Jackson. Both candidates were black. Campbell's campaign centred on the tax issue. Lomax lost in the city. Fulton County, meanwhile, elected a white candidate, Mitch Skandalakis, to the chair after he defeated Martin Luther King III.

High profile jobs conceal old divides

The economic gap between black workers and white workers widened between 1980 and 1990. White unemployment was much lower, down from 4.4 to 3.5% during that period. By contrast, 13% of African Americans were unemployed in 1990. Income inequality was pronounced. In 1980, the incomes of black people fell from 63% of that of their white colleagues to 56% in 1990. Black infant mortality rates, meanwhile, were four times as high as for white infants.[21]

Despite such statistics, black people still see Atlanta as a sort of Mecca. One-third of the black population in Atlanta has lived there for less than five years. Black people talk about the city as being a laboratory where white and black co-operation is tested. Socially, and in the workplace, the races are mixing more. But residential areas are more exclusively one or the other. It is colour which defines where a person lives rather than class in the sense that middle-class blacks live in one suburb, and middle-class whites in another. But some of the poorest districts are almost 100% minority population, effectively meaning black.

Big companies in the city positively promote minorities to jobs which have a public profile. When the business community hosted a welcome lunch downtown for Maynard Jackson as he took office in 1990, companies were careful to send along their black and other minority management. The senior posts in big companies are still occupied mostly by whites. Some blacks decide to leave the corporations when promotion is slow and set up on their own. Atlanta's black middle-class tradition is reflected partially in a few big black-owned companies. The city ranked sixth in the number of its black-owned firms in a survey of metropolitan areas carried out by the Bureau of the Census in 1987, and topped the list measured by the average annual revenue per firm. But for every bit of evidence that educated blacks setting up their own businesses are making progress, another clue to the difficulties that they encounter is revealed. In a survey of 150 black-owned businesses in Atlanta, three-quarters reported that they had encountered discrimination while trying to get finance from the banks.[22]

The minorities population is growing more rapidly than the overall population in the Atlanta Region, the black population twice as fast, while the Hispanic population more than doubled between 1980 and 1990, and Asians increased by more than four times. Over 70 000 Hispanics and Asians moved into the area in that time, although they were still only 4% of the population in 1990. Legal and illegal immigrants from these territories frequently work in low-paid jobs in catering and hotels which have expanded rapidly as part of the growing convention business and tourism in the city.

The perceived threat from newer minorities

Asians and Hispanics are doing work similar to that taken by the black population a generation ago, and potentially are an economic threat to poorer blacks. The record in other American cities which have a much longer experience of immigration from these areas is that many will progress rapidly up the economic ladder, leaving behind increasingly embittered young black males without work. Speaking at the Atlanta History Society seminar on race, however, Reverend Reynell Parkins, preacher in an Episcopalian church downtown that has a wealthy, white, black and Hispanic congregation, predicted that class rather than race was becoming the dominant issue in the city.

The struggle in Atlanta is no longer between middle and upper class blacks and poor blacks, but between poor whites and poor blacks against middle and upper class blacks and whites.

A city too busy to hate – the development of Atlanta's race relations

The history of Atlanta, however, never strays far from race, and the white businessmen who shaped the growth of the city. By the early part of the century, government and the business community were pretty well inter-twined. Senior businessmen would nominate their candidates for political office and pay their campaign costs. They were chosen purely and simply to move the business agenda.

The race question, however, could not be ignored. William Hartsfield as mayor is credited with having coined the phrase that 'Atlanta was a city too busy to hate.' During his terms of office in the 1940s the contacts with the black leadership, and deals, were made. The City deliberately expanded its white population by annexing some of the northern suburbs while the black leadership agreed to its community being restricted to certain districts in return for land destined to be used for middle-class black housing.[23]

The ground was also being prepared for the federal investment which was to come later, and which eventually totalled over $6 billion in urban renewal, MARTA, Hartsfield airport and new expressways. Harry West, executive director of the Atlanta Regional Commission, summed it up:

Atlanta had people with vision. It is what has distinguished the city. It was not altruism, it was what was good for business, and it meant looking ahead, anticipating the next set of problems. A metropolitan planning commission was recommended in 1938. The freeway system was based on a transport study commissioned postwar. The airport expanded with resources going on runways rather than fancy term-inals, in place for when the big jets arrived. Hartsville pioneered the hub concept. In 1954, a plan was drawn up for the public ownership of the bus system, and for a subway, again ready to implement when the money was available.[24]

Racial violence in the 1960s could have wrecked the plans, and that would have set back Atlanta's development by a generation. The mayor during most of that decade – 1961 to 1969 – was Ivan Allen. With a few key figures, this white businessman struggled against his segregationist colleagues on the council. 'Mayor Allen appointed a bi-racial committee to increase jobs opportunities for blacks, and, in 1963, at the request of President Kennedy, he testified in favour of the newly introduced federal civil-rights bill.'[25] He was the only mayor in the South openly to support the bill in that way. Robert Woodruff, the Coca-Cola magnate, worked behind the scenes to persuade business colleagues to back measures designed to improve opportunities for blacks. On the issue of desegregation, his advice was: 'Clearly this is the situation and we have to work with it . . . If he had said fight it, it would have been Birmingham, Alabama all over again.'[26]

Atlanta then had already got a reputation for being liberal relative to the rest of the South. Disillusionment, however, could set in fast. A black woman recalled how she had arrived in the city, and was travelling in a yellow taxi-cab when it was rammed by a car. She was barred by the white occupants from going any further. 'You won't go beyond here', she was told.[27]

The 1960s were the turning point in the balance of the unofficial coalition of white and black middle class. Businessmen from that period talk today about their colleagues' 'enlightened self-interest' in recognizing that the demands of the black community were being changed by civil rights and the emergence of younger, more militant black leaders. Although some of this new leadership

> had only transitory roles . . . the new black establishment . . . became more assertive. During Ivan Allen's two terms as mayor, discord beset the governing coalition. On the one side, the white business elite, long accustomed to calling the shots in civic affairs, seemed tempted to disregard new elements and demands. Only sustained protests led them to end the exclusion of blacks from public accommodations in downtown Atlanta. When civil disorders generated new policy priorities, the business elite still held back; they failed to support a bond issue to fund a systematic program of neighbourhood development. The mayor's housing proposal fared little better.[28]

The MARTA project was highlighted by Clarence Stone as an example of how the business elite worked, giving way only when stubbornness threatened the total plan. MARTA had to win federal funding if it was to go ahead, and that was not finally until 1972, when voters in the two central counties agreed to a sales tax which attracted matching funds. MARTA had a highly controversial gestation period.

> The members and chair of MARTA's board of directors were all business executives. Not surprisingly, MARTA was frequently charged with unresponsive arrogance and in 1968 its first attempt to gain voter approval of the system's financing was rejected . . . In 1972, after the federal government's agreement to finance most of the system, an intensive public relations campaign, and route changes sought by the black community, voters were persuaded to approve the project.[29]

After the death of Martin Luther King, the Action Forum was set up with the help of more progressive business players to promote blacks into the boardrooms and higher echelons of white business. This was apart from the black business sector which catered mostly for black clients, and dated from the turn of the century by which time some former slaves who had set up in Atlanta had made money, and bought property. Banks and insurance services were started by entrepreneurs who endowed the city with Atlanta Life Insurance, one of the largest black-owned stockholder life insurance companies, and Citizens Trust Company.

Another initiative dating from 1969 was Leadership Atlanta, set up by the Chamber of Commerce to bring together people with different racial and professional backgrounds and familiarize them with the different sectors of the city. They would then go back to their communities with a special responsibility and understanding of the city. The scheme has been picked up by many American cities since. Atlanta also has a Regional Leadership Institute, with broadly similar aims but covering a wider territory.

The rise of a prospering black city

The City of Atlanta was changing in many respects. Its black educational institutions were preferred by black students from all over the country to mixed race universities and colleges. The City was becoming a black city. It made an attempt to expand its boundaries in 1972; this was challenged in the courts and pronounced unconstitutional. Allen had turned out to be the last but one of the line of white business-nominated mayors. Maynard Jackson was elected in 1973, the first black mayor. White enrolment in city public schools then preparing to be desegregated had been falling dramatically, to 23% of the total in 1972–73, against 59% ten years earlier.

Jackson turned out to be a significant leader, although he was a controversial leader in the eyes of the business community. He had not come out of the black political elite, and was determined to demonstrate his independence from the sort of alliances that had propped up past mayors, while promoting black economic progress. He ushered in the Minority Business Enterprise programme, which required that 35% of City placed contracts go to minority businesses directly, or through contracts or subcontracts, or in joint ventures with minority partners. It was the time that work was due to start on the airport expansion and on building the subway. The business groups objected, but the measure was passed. He also set up the Atlanta Economic Development Corporation aimed at job creation through public and private partnerships.

The business community found the Jackson reform agenda difficult to live with. But Jackson's achievements fell well short of his ambitions.

As mayor, Jackson's bold assertion of a reform agenda was based on the assumption that he had a popular mandate to lead in that direction. After all, he was a capable exerciser of the formal authority of the office, and as a popular leader, he was able to mobilize mass support. But he lacked command of the informal system of cooperation that was so important in the civic life of Atlanta.[30]

Andrew Young returned to Atlanta in 1981 as the new mayor after serving as President Carter's ambassador to the United Nations. He excelled in the role of ambassador of Atlanta, particularly overseas 'setting the stage for Atlanta to become an international player'.[31] Although he was elected without the support of the business community, he negotiated a new understanding between City Hall and the big downtown corporations in particular. The business leaders chose to see the process as black leadership being able to take more mature decisions than in the first flush of power.

Waking up to recession

Maynard Jackson returned in 1989 to serve a third term. He took over Young's representational mantle with enthusiasm, and pledged to shore up the ailing services provided by the City. Pride in MARTA could not detract from some of the most crime-ridden public housing projects in the country and an atmosphere of declining public safety. Jackson brought in trouble-shooters to sort out some of the problem areas, among them Earl Phillips to run the Atlanta Housing Authority. Phillips had acquired a reputation in other cities for instilling order into public housing projects, evicting families if necessary if they were consistently in crime, while softening the heavy hand of bureaucracy to encourage other tenants in showing some pride and responsibility in the projects.

Both the business community and Jackson were looking for a better working relationship than they had had in the 1970s. But Jackson was unlucky, and ran into

> the realities of very difficult economic conditions – the previous 10 years had been a roll for Atlanta, then it got caught up in the same troubles as the rest of the country. Jackson could not do what he wanted. There were too many promises, too big an agenda, and not enough accomplished. But he represented the city well nationally and internationally.[32]

Jackson did not stand again four years later. Campbell, a lawyer who Jackson backed as his successor, was not the business community's choice. But the signals were gathering that the pendulum was swinging back towards business acting as the catalyst for some of the long overdue reforms in the way that the City's services were being managed. The private-sector leadership saw the pay-off in potentially more efficient management of basic services, like water supplies and disposal of solid waste. Contracting-out of services to the private sector by the City, for example, had been minimal so far. The worsening financial position of the City might hinder, or might help push through changes.

2.6 BUSINESS AND POLITICAL PARTNERSHIPS

The business elite has never been far from the major civic decisions in Atlanta, even in later years. The dominant motivation for business in working with civic leaders has always been self-interest. The extent to which this co-operation constituted a partnership in the true sense that business itself would understand – that both partners share the risks – was not always apparent.

Urban renewal – once a handsome pay-off for private business

Urban renewal marked a highly controversial period in Atlanta's history. The normal pattern in American cities was that neighbourhoods were declared by the council to be in decline, clearance followed, land was assembled for sale at a subsidized price to the developer. The developers benefited, as did the council, when high-priced and high-rented housing and other properties replaced the poor dwellings and yielded higher taxes. The implication was that developers could hardly lose. 'Urban renewal is a gamble for small stakes with a fortune if the cards fall right and a small loss if they fall wrong'.[33]

One neighbourhood in Atlanta stands out among many across the city as an example of the sweeping powers invested in the politicians. Summerhill has attracted more attention than most because it is the site of Fulton County Stadium, which was part of Atlanta's bid to get into the top baseball league and is home to the Atlanta Braves team. The Olympics Stadium is scheduled to be built there.

Summerhill was not a slum back in the 1950s. But the community's recollection is that white and black leaders conspired to emphasize that the area was declining fast, so that they could ignore suggestions from community groups on how that decline might be halted. The area took its first hit from the clearances which were to make way for a new expressway. Douglas Dean, brought up in Summerhill, and leader of one of the neighbourhood development organizations in the area, explained:

That took between 5000 and 6000 people away, and some very good houses. In the 1960s, the stadium took out another 5000 to 6000.

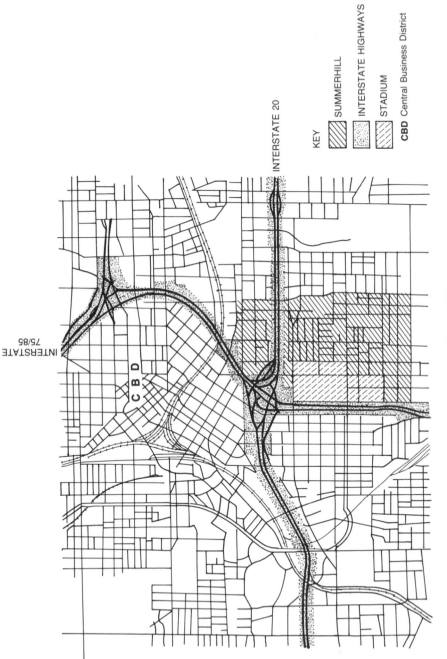

INTERSTATE
75/85

C B D

INTERSTATE 20

KEY

SUMMERHILL

INTERSTATE HIGHWAYS

STADIUM

CBD Central Business District

Figure 2.7 The district of Summerhill in relation to central Atlanta, 1990.

Summerhill had been a very strong community of around 20 000, black and white, and Jewish . . . After this, the [Federal] Model Cities Programme came along to re-build neighbourhoods like Summerhill. Basically, nothing really happened. The money could not be leveraged up. The financial institutions would not invest in the community.[34]

Summerhill over the years has seen several schemes planted on it. The latest development of modestly priced private housing, however, is the first stage in a strategy to upgrade the quality of life in the area. The plans were worked up by the community in conjunction with leading public and private sector players and charitable groups in the city. They aim to promote business development, quality employment, education, and training, and goods and services at affordable prices, as well as 'spiritual life enhancement'.[35]

The 1960s Federal urban renewal grants gave way to more targeted forms of grant aid and to measures like tax increment financing, which ploughs back the enhanced values of property in a new development into retiring a bond. Urban renewal can still be controversial in Atlanta, however. The Olympic Village was planned for the campus of Georgia Institute of Technology. It could be the catalyst for new private housing in the area of Techwood Homes, the problem public housing project opposite the campus and adjacent to the new commercial centre in the Midtown area, but it aroused suspicion and opposition from those who saw themselves being manipulated by the Olympics organizers.

Two American studies on urban elites in American cities concluded that the politicians were often no match for the weight of the development lobby. They may well have had their election campaigns financed by the lobby. 'Campaign contributions remain the mother's milk of United States politics' which at the local level 'come overwhelmingly from growth machine sectors' (defined as 'an apparatus of interlocking pro-growth associations and governmental units').[36] Growth machine activists are

largely free of concern for what goes on within production processes (for example, occupational safety), for the actual use-value of the products made locally (for example, cigarettes) or for spillover consequences in the lives of residents (for example, pollution). They tend to oppose any intervention that might regulate development on behalf of use-values. They may quarrel among themselves over exactly how rents will be distributed among parcels, over how, that is, they will share the spoils of aggregate growth. But virtually all place entrepreneurs and their growth machine associates, regardless of geographical or social location, easily agree on the issue of growth itself.[37]

Central Atlanta Progress (CAP)

CAP is a powerful organization representing the big downtown corporations in Atlanta, set up in 1941, says its literature, 'to work with each other and with government to build a better central city'. CAP from the start was much more than another lobby group. It quickly became an integral part of the planning process in Atlanta. Its membership comprises the chairpersons and CEOs of companies and institutions which are invited by the board of directors to join CAP. Despite the desertion of the central area by many major companies over the last 20 years, its membership still reads like a rollcall of the Atlanta greats. Its organizational powers have helped prise funds from government. It has close links with the office of mayor, and city personnel. Politicians and business come together with differing perspectives on their goals, but the goal of sustaining the central City is the same.

CAP has undertaken two major planning exercises jointly with the City on the central area, the first worked up in the 1960s, the second in the 1980s, which is directed at turning a part of the declining lower down-

Figure 2.8 Downtown Atlanta: business prosperity at the centre disguises poverty in the inner suburbs. *Courtesy of Atlanta Chamber of Commerce.*

town into a centre of government offices for the City and the county, and state and federal offices.

The best-known Atlanta development downtown was at the city end of Peachtree Street, starting with the Hyatt Regency Hotel, one of the first of the atria-designs which later proliferated in buildings across the United States and Europe. Peachtree Centre, also to the design of local architect John Portman, came later. Portman, president of CAP in 1971, was 'the country's new whiz kid of architecture . . . Atlanta was the new urban star, and Atlanta was the city John Portman was building'.[38]

CAP helped to propel investment downtown with the help of public subsidies. Members included financial institutions which could be hauled in to put together partnership deals that would be outside the scope of more conventional partnerships. One example was Underground Atlanta, opened in 1989 as a festival shopping complex which became quickly a downtown landmark close to the busiest MARTA intersection. The Rouse company which created market type shopping in old districts of cities around the world, has a share in running this project.

An earlier entertainment complex had opened in this complex of streets and railroad depot in the city which went below ground when the street system was elevated in the 1920s. But it closed when the subway was put through the district. CAP played a critical role in garnering public finance and tax breaks for individuals in putting together the deal for the new Underground.

> The case of Underground suggests that a unified and powerful business elite, attractive to and allied with an activist mayor (Young), and a program of minority business participation whereby legislative support can be courted are the central elements in a governing coalition that works – one that can move along even enormously complex, costly, and controversial projects.[39]

The Georgia Dome stadium opened three years later in another downtown area which needed an extra anchor and close to the Congress Convention Centre which marked Atlanta's entry into what proved to be a successful addition to the central city economy. The Georgia Dome is a new sporting complex which was financed in part by a sales tax on hotel stays agreed by the state. It is home to the Atlanta Falcons, and in January 1994 it hosted the nation's football Super Bowl. It was estimated that in return for $3m put up by the city, county, state, and business, the four-day weekend event would generate up to $135m spent by 70 000 visitors.

Scaling down regeneration projects

Downtown activity was focusing on smaller projects in the 1990s. They included Georgia State University's developing new downtown centre of culture; conversion of the Atlanta jail into a federal detention centre and a new, much larger city jail; conversion of Rich's closed department store building into a complex for federal government employees; improvement of Woodruff Park; and, most ambitious, but dependent on state funding, would be a 'multi-modal' transportation centre linking local and interstate rail and bus services, to be sited at Five Points.

CAP is involved in projects in the downtown with the City to improve safety. A security communications network was set up with the Atlanta Police Department and private security forces to improve public safety, for example. But the future of downtown remains uncertain. 'Atlanta is on its third wave of development. There are more and more "edge cities" on the perimeter highway and along the radial spokes' – there had been pressure in the mid 1970s that jobs should be located outside the city as a way of cutting the distances that commuters travelled. Now, of course, people have moved further out. 'We are not trying to compete for every new headquarters but to develop it for government, tourism, higher education, conventions, residential for upper and middle income households, student accommodation and workspace.'[40]

Atlanta has no tradition of downtown living. It is characterized by the planning priority that was given to the automobile, now being slowly remedied. Underground Atlanta and Georgia Dome are employment replacements for the corporations which have moved north to the high rise buildings in Midtown, and to Buckhead and suburbs strung out along the interstate Highways 75 and 85 and Highway 400. Whether the downtown can hang on with its new order of activities is uncertain, notwithstanding CAP, the Atlanta Downtown Partnership, and other players.

Populist power demands a new way forward

Business decisions on location and the lure of the suburbs for families have been prime factors in shaping the physical expansion of Atlanta. In this sense, they do indeed

> help determine just where economic activities are to be situated, and what social and environmental conditions accompany such activities. Their participation, whether successful or not for their own growth goals, is the link between the local community and cosmopolitan capital.[41]

The growth of Atlanta has additional implications. The cohesive elite which staged the grand projects of the past is no more. That there was a 'concentration of power in a relatively few economic hands presumably means there is less capacity for competing groups to frustrate leadership action'.[42] Community groups, property owners, and particularly the poorer members of society were swept aside in the tidal wave of the business elite's plans, although there were concessions from the more philanthropic-minded corporate and civic heads. But CEOs are now spread all around the region, and their strategic efforts are directed towards taking their corporations into the twenty-first century. 'You cannot pull these companies together if you are going on a fund-raising event' was the wry comment of one businessman close to the old guard.

The worrying aspect of that statement is that the social problems have not gone away. The social mayhem produced by the wave of addiction to crack cocaine far outstrips the charitable capacity of city churches and foundations, which have been the traditional helpers when the state does not provide.

Vision 2020

The quality of the environment and the rule of the automobile are major concerns for the future shape of Atlanta. The Atlanta Regional Commission (ARC) is designated by Georgia law as the comprehensive planning agency for the region in the areas of transportation, land use, the environment, and human services. Its powers are limited, however, so it is trying to establish a new format to guide Atlanta's development by involving 'all of the Atlanta Region's people in choosing a preferred future for the Region and developing a plan that will take us there'.[43] 'We are being forced to accept the fact that it is a populist power structure, which is more diverse, more spread out geographically, and involves a lot more people', said Harry West, executive director.[44]

George Busbee, former Georgia Governor, agreed to head the steering committee. He said in 1992: 'Federal government has withdrawn, the state is going broke, Atlanta is going to have to regionally address its own problems.'[45] A partner in a leading Atlanta law firm, he sees Atlanta's future as tied up in its goal to be an international region.

The nine counties region covers 2584 square miles and includes 57 cities. Metropolitan Atlanta, as defined for the Census, has 20 counties, over 100 cities, covers 6150 square miles. 'What is difficult as you try to address all these problems is to look at maps; all you see is boundaries'.[46]

The plan will encompass economic, physical and human resources within a framework calculated to reverse the growth pressures which are causing massive deterioration of the environment. Nature may actually take its own course. Development in this part of Georgia could be severely limited by the availability of water. Over 80% of the region's water comes from the Chattahoochee River, which the authorities are trying desperately to protect from development and other land-disturbing activities.[47] Atlanta has also been in dispute with the neighbouring state of Alabama since 1990, and more recently with Florida, over the release of water from two lakes in the area.

Vision 2020 is in two parts: the population was asked, via a survey inserted in local newspapers, to articulate their vision for the region, which was distilled and published. The next stage will be to identify the policies, projects and procedures to make the vision become real. The final plan will then be published in late 1995. Ten functional areas have been picked, ranging from health and human services, to transportation, and the economy. The policy for each will be steered by a committee of between 10 and 15, who will identify and recruit 80–90 'stakeholders', and then assess the resources that will be needed. Stakeholders will make it their job to see that plans will be implemented.

> We are turning the business of the people back to the people. As far as we know it is unique. We don't know if it will work. We do know that time, circumstances are changing. We have to try to do new things. With the right mix of people, and over a period of time, they will have generated enough support for their recommen-dations that there will be a groundswell of people saying: take us there.[48]

Georgia Research Alliance – feeding Atlanta's role in high technology

Corporate relocation has become a significant part of Atlanta's economic growth. Now more effort perhaps needs to be put into organic growth, in particular to expand and develop the high-technology base in sectors where the city has a head start, and to use technology more widely to upgrade traditional industries.

Georgia is not a high-tech state. There is no Silicon Valley, Route 128, or Research Triangle equivalent. Georgia has been competing for incom-ing investment – national and international – which was attracted by non-unionized labour, good communications, low wages, and space. The drawback is that another state, another country, can always be found that will do it more cheaply. Georgia is also losing some of its traditional industry sectors which cannot meet the more demanding environmental requirements.

Against this background, the Georgia Research Alliance was launched in 1990 to raise the profile of technology and its applications. It was to work with service industries as well as manufacturing, and to capitalize on the research institutions located in the state. Telecommunications, media and entertainment were an obvious starting point. Atlanta has inter-nationally recognized companies in broadcasting, computers, tele-communications, consumer electronics and cable television, including AT & T, Bell South, Scientific-Atlanta (cable television and satellite equip-

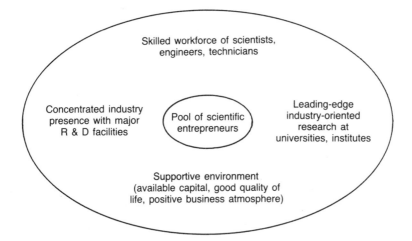

Figure 2.9 Moving towards critical mass: the goal of the Georgia Research Alliance.
Source: Technology, Innovation and Regional Economic Development – Background Paper No. 2, Congressional Office of Technology Assessment, 1983; McKinsey interviews.

ment), Cox Communications, Hayes Microcomputer Products (communications software), CNN and others.

The Atlanta region is also home to six universities, specializing in different areas of basic and applied research, of which Georgia Institute of Technology is best known internationally. By bringing them closer together, Atlanta is bidding to become a national centre in telecommunications through the formation of the Georgia Centre for Advanced Telecommunications Technology, under the auspices of the Georgia Research Alliance.

The germ of the idea for the Alliance came from the Woodruff Foundation. State Governor Zel Miller was anxious to get some consistency into Georgia's uneven attempts to stimulate research and development. The core funding of $18.8m came from the state and business and was to be leveraged up by the private sector as and when its research plans were hatched.

The Alliance itself acts partly as broker between business and academic institutions. Its mixed parentage enables it to act as a forum where the universities can play down the traditional rivalry for research funds. The Board of CEOs and university presidents picked a director who describes himself as 'fifth-generation Georgian, fourth-generation Atlantan', whose knowledge of the region has helped in putting together partnerships. Research is intended to be publicly beneficial as well as having commercial spin-off. One example is Telemedicine, a communications system which allows doctors to diagnose medical conditions in a patient in rural areas up to 130 miles distant. Distance learning is planned in inner-city schools.

Top researchers from centres around the country are recruited who contract with the company which wants a particular research project to be carried out on its behalf. The research is directed within the university, however, where the researcher is given a tenured post to run a section.

Traditional industries like textiles, pulp and paper, and food processing have been targeted. 'Technology-driven economic development is at the root of our national competitiveness', says William Todd, president, Georgia Research Alliance.[49] Pulp and paper, and carpets are two traditional sectors in Georgia under environmental pressure unless the companies can apply new technology to upgrade their methods of manufacture. Over two-thirds of carpets made in the United States are made in Georgia, of which about a third are exported. Customers want increasingly sophisticated dyes which call for very high temperatures. A new sensor control technology permitted one manufacturer to cut the period needed for the dyeing process without damaging the colour. The upgraded process consumes less energy, and Atlanta does not have to deal with river pollution. And a venture capital fund put together by local banks and finance houses is to be launched to back new new research-based companies.

2.7 THE ATLANTA MESSAGE

Atlanta has a well-earned reputation among American cities for boosterism, with such propaganda Forward Atlanta puts out:

> What makes this city special? Maybe it's the inherent geographical advantages that make Atlanta so attractive. It could be the superior international airport, or the robust international community that is growing and thriving here. Possibly, it is the incredible spirit of cooperation and progressive leadership that has grown out of the seat of the civil rights movement . . .

Despite the blight of poverty, the message to the world is that Atlanta has something special to offer, and that public and private partnerships have worked in the city. This was certainly an important factor in the Olympics bid.

NOTES

1. Best cities for business (1992) *Fortune*.
2. *Atlanta Region Outlook* (1993) Atlanta Regional Commission.

3. Ibid.
4. Economic Forecast Unit (1994) Georgia State University.
5. Joel Cowan, chairman, Cowan & Associates, in interview with the author, February 1994.
6. Leinberger, Christopher B. and Lockwood, Charles (1986) How business is reshaping America, *Atlantic Monthly*, **258**(4), October.
7. Ibid.
8. *Atlanta Journal*, 16 February 1994.
9. *Because There is Hope* (1993) A Report of the Atlanta Project.
10. *A Shared Vision for the Atlanta Region* (1993) Atlanta Regional Commission.
11. Dan Sweat, Director of TAP, in interview with the author, 1994.
12. Ibid.
13. Donald Ratajcak (1992) Centre for Economic Forecasting, Georgia State University, in interview with the German-Marshall Fund team, 1992.
14. *Report of Recommendations* (1991) Georgia Partnership for Excellence in Education.
15. *Atlanta Journal*, 19 February 1994.
16. Stone, C. F. (1989) *Regime Politics*, University Press of Kansas.
17. Atlanta briefing material prepared for the German-Marshall Fund Team, 1992.
18. Interview with the German-Marshall Fund Team, 1992.
19. Forward Atlanta (1992) *Get the Facts* brochure.
20. Interview with the German-Marshall Fund team, 1992.
21. *Status of Black Atlanta* (1994) Southern Center for Studies in Public Policy, Clark Atlanta University.
22. Black entrepreneurialism, *Wall Street Journal* special section, 3 April 1992.
23. Stone, *Regime Politics*, op. cit.
24. Interview with the German-Marshall Fund team, 1992.
25. Stone, *Regime Politics*, op. cit.
26. Joel Cowan, in interview with the author, 1994, paraphrasing Woodruff.
27. Veronica Clayton,. Corporate vice president for urban affairs, Turner Broadcasting Systems, speaking at a seminar, 1994
28. Stone, *Regime Politics*, op. cit.
29. Tabb, W. K. and Sawers, L. (eds) (1984) *Marxism and the Metropolis*, 2nd edn, New York: Oxford University Press. Quoted in Logan, J. R. and Molotch, H. L. (1987) *Urban Fortunes*, University of California Press.
30. Stone, *Regime Politics*, op. cit.
31. Kelman, P. B., Vice president Central Atlanta Progress Inc., in interview with the author, 1994.
32. Ibid.
33. Abrams, C. (1967) *The City is the Frontier*, Harper Colophon.
34. Interview with the German-Marshall Fund team, 1992.
35. Goldman Sachs (no date) *Summerhill: A Community Revitalization*.
36. Molotch, H. L. (1976) The city as a growth machine, *American Journal of Sociology*.
37. Logan, J. R. and Molotch, H. L. (1987) *Urban Fortunes: The Political Economy of Place*, University of California Press.
38. Gratz, R. B. (1990) *The Living City*, Simon & Schuster.

39. Stone, *Regime Politics, op. cit.*
40. Kelman, interview with author, *op. cit.*
41. Cummings, S. (ed) (1988) *Business Elites and Urban Development*, State University of New York.
42. Ibid.
43. Atlanta Regional Commission (1993) *Vision 2020.*
44. Interview with the author, 1994.
45. Interview with the German-Marshall Fund Team, 1992.
46. Ibid.
47. *Outlook* (1993) Atlanta Regional Commission.
48. Harry West, in interview with the author, 1994.
49. Interview with the author, 1994.

Birmingham

3

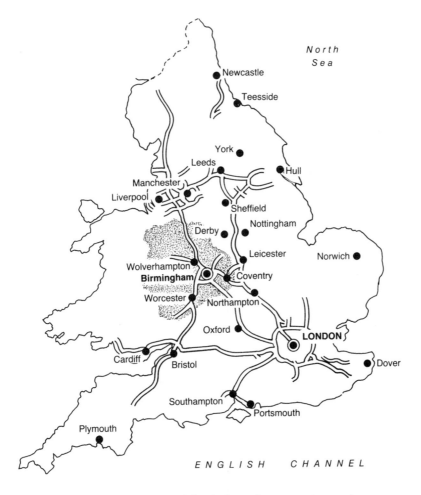

Figure 3.1 The West Midlands (═══ denotes motorways).

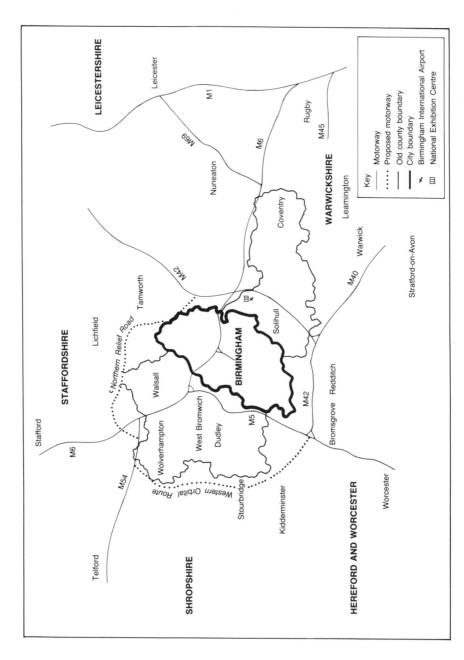

Figure 3.2 Birmingham within the Midlands.

Table 3.1 Basic facts about Birmingham

(a) Population

West Midlands region	Conurbation[1]	Birmingham
5.2m	2.6m	961 000

Note: 1. Old West Midlands County Council.

Source: Census, 1991.

(b) Ethnic minorities

Birmingham	Conurbation[1]
21.6%	14.6%

Note: 1. Old West Midlands County Council.

(c) Percentage of public housing in Birmingham: 26.4%

(d) Percentage of working-age population with university degree:
     8.6% (W Midlands County)

(e) Employment: see Figures 3.4 and 3.5.

(f) Unemployment, mid 1994

Birmingham	Conurbation[1]
17.4%	11.4%

Note: 1. Old West Midlands County Council.

(g) Top five corporations (by employment), Birmingham region

1. Rover
2. British Telecom
3. Cadbury Schweppes
4. West Midlands Travel
5. Lloyds Bank

3.1 INTRODUCTION

Britain's workshop

'Today, only two cities remain economically vigorous and prosperous. One is London. The second is Birmingham.' So wrote Jane Jacobs in *The Economy of Cities*, in 1968.[1] Her verdict on British cities betrayed her fascination with the entrepreneurial style that had been the hallmark of Birmingham. In the nineteenth century, the city had developed an economy which proved more resilient than that of Manchester, its great rival. Manchester was dominated by a single industry, cotton textiles. The organization of the industry was an example of large-scale production and economies of scale.

By contrast, the Birmingham economy was made up of a mass of small firms, making a wide range of goods, mostly, but certainly not exclusively, by shaping metals. Birmingham prospered as long as its goods were internationally competitive. This may not have been the era of the global economy, but the health of Birmingham business depended on the cycles of world trade. Wars were good for its economy. So was the expansion of the British Empire with its protected markets. But firms came under pressure if their products could be made more cheaply elsewhere. The chamber of commerce was complaining bitterly in the 1870s about the impossibility of competing with Germany in making bolts and screws. Firms would go under or adapt, new firms were born, preparing and shaping metal to produce new items. It was known as 'the city of a thousand trades'. Most Birmingham goods were produced in volume. Even more craft-based industries like jewellery-making and goldsmithing were often more interested in quantity than quality. Despite efforts by some leading businessmen to preach the commercial wisdom of high quality and sound reputation, most of the goods produced were of relatively low value. Many products were components.

> What was going on in Birmingham at a great rate, as opposed to Manchester, was much trial and error, sometimes leading to successful new activities and sometimes not . . . Viewing the city's economy as a whole, one can think of it as a great, confused economic laboratory, supporting itself by its own production. Of course, taken as a whole, it was also inefficient.[2]

The theory was that specialization, as practised in Manchester's textiles, while efficient, was ultimately ruinous since so much was invested in the fortunes of one industry. Diversity as demonstrated by Birmingham, allowed the economy to go on developing. The evolution of industry from cycle to motor production, for decades now the mainstay, is a case in point. Business in the city may have complained about foreign competition – indeed it still does – but there was a dynamism which was not paralleled in cities and towns more dependent on a narrow range of employment.

The early entrepreneurs included some of the great innovators: John Baskerville in the eighteenth century turned to printing after he had made his fortune elsewhere, inventing a typeface which is still one of the most used in English language publications; Matthew and Boulton pioneered the application of steam to power machines. Industrial dynasties were created: Lucas of lamp fame and now an international motor and aerospace components group; Nettlefold which, from a base of nuts and bolts, turned itself into GKN and derives a staple income from one of the critical components which makes possible the production of front-wheel drive cars; Austin whose small car provided the starting point for the latter-day revival of the Japanese motor industry and is one of the antecedent companies of Rover Cars; Cadbury whose chocolate-making was the base for what became the international food and drinks group, Cadbury-Schweppes. Although best-known for its engineering technologies, Birmingham was the birthplace of Lloyds and Midland, two of the UK's largest joint stock banks.

The entrepreneurialism and innovativeness of nineteenth-century Birmingham were just the characteristics which Mrs Margaret Thatcher, as prime minister, wanted to replant in British industry during the 1980s. But Birmingham, still the heart of UK manufacturing, by then seemed no longer to be providing the entrepreneurs.

Amalgamations, mergers and asset-stripping hit the city in the 1960s and early 1970s. Family-run engineering companies frequently lacked investment. Their owners were often willing victims to the financial predators. The motor industry had been pushed back into narrower and narrower markets. The Austin car plant in the Birmingham suburb of Longbridge had been subsumed into the British Motor Corporation, which became British Leyland. That group was rescued by the government but only by the late 1980s was it able to recapture domestic and international competitiveness. The British taxpayer footed the bill for a return to stability, but the consumer, meanwhile, had long since been won over to continental European cars which were often cheaper and more stylish, and, later, to Japanese cars which were of greater reliability. All this mattered desperately to the component makers in and around Birmingham; their health was crucially dependent on the health of the troubled indigenous motor industry.

By the early 1980s, in any case, the sterling exchange rate, buoyed by Britain's North Sea oil reserves, made Britain's exports uncompetitive. Sir Michael Edwardes, head of British Leyland, won spirited applause for his plea to the government to ease the damage that was being done to British manufacturing. Addressing the national conference of the Confederation of British Industry, he argued that it might be better to 'leave the bloody stuff [N Sea oil] in the ground'.

What had seemed a source of strength to Jacobs in the 1960s, with her grasp of historical perspective, looked an eroded asset in the 1980s.

When the Midlands' share in a shrinking world market for cars was eroded from the 1970s, its virtues of small independent production were exposed as fiction. The car industry's success had reduced umpteen companies to tie themselves to it. Each car contained hundreds of parts, some manufactured by firms employing several thousands, others by small producers employing a couple of score. These component suppliers suffered from domino decline. Success in the Midlands motor and electrical industries thus eventually bred the same vices that the north-west's textile industry suffered from earlier.[3]

Birmingham suffered less than other parts of the West Midlands region. Coventry at the south-eastern end, home of Jaguar cars, and other types of vehicle assembly, was devastated. Wrapping Birmingham on the north and west is a string of industrial towns, with myriad activities from locks to chains and steel to glass crystal-making, called the Black Country. Heavy industry in the area was swept by closures in the early 1980s. Birmingham, however, had a higher proportion of service employment than these towns. Indeed, it is the financial centre not only for the Birmingham–Black Country conurbation but also the region as a whole, the nearest available source of banking, insurance, accounting and legal services on any scale. But Birmingham was still highly dependent in 1980 on manufacturing both for the direct work it provided and for the business it provided for the service and professional firms of the city. By August 1984, 20% of the workforce was registered as unemployed, and 46% of the unemployed had not worked for over a year.

The Birmingham city council had already been trying, within the limited scope available, to stimulate the economy. There was nothing surprising in that. Municipal intervention in the local economy had strong precedents, dating back to the 1870s, the heyday of Joseph Chamberlain, arguably one of the strongest local government leaders of the last 150 years.

Chamberlain remains a mentor of contemporary local leaders. A businessman who made a fortune before he entered Birmingham politics, he created his reputation for enlightened city government on the principle that the public sector should provide basic services for the population of the city, like water, sewerage and housing. With proper provision for the people who made up the workforce, he believed the private sector could flourish. (It was on the back of his reputation that he went into national politics as a Liberal, who later became a Unionist.) Chamberlain and his colleagues were responsible for an early bout of urban renewal. 'One of Chamberlain's objectives in building Corporation Street, apart from clearing a slum area, had been to extend the range of the town's main shopping streets.'[4] In sweeping away the slums, he saw the opportunity to boost the city's income from services. The new street 'radically altered the whole topography of central Birmingham'.[5]

A century later, the thinking of Birmingham's political leaders again drifted in the direction of boosting the service economy. It was a natural course, given that the city is the centre of the region, even it it was not original. Many, if not most, north European and North American industrial cities were thinking along the same lines. Whether it would have been better to work harder at holding on to and succouring the industrial companies in the city, many of which have left the city in the last ten years, will not be proved.

The city leaders decided that to boost the services economy, the city would have to offer a more appealing physical face to the world. Aesthetically, it was a poor relation of most second-tier continental European cities, let alone capitals. Its inner areas had been brutalized by the angularity of 1960s buildings, although the townscape had been praised at the time. In their search for modernity and better living conditions, city officials seem to have been very good at persuading the government not only that it should subsidize a massive spending spree on new tower block housing in the 1960s and '70s, that proved disastrously unsuitable for the families rehoused in them, but also that it should back ambitious new road plans. Birmingham at least would come to terms with the motor car: it made them, it should be able to live with them. The planners, under the influence of Sir Herbert Manzoni, who was the city engineer said to have been the architect of post-war Birmingham, believed this was the best way forward for what was then a very prosperous industrial city. They can now be seen to have displayed the characteristic disregard of officials in those days for the dignity of the people who lived there, many of whom did not have motor cars.

Two ring roads were built, one to encircle the centre, the other around the inner city. The central ring, completed in 1971 and opened by the Queen, was the obvious mark of accommodation with the motor car. Pedestrians, however, had to get across the city by weaving their way through a series of underpasses. The inner ring road served its purpose in de-congesting the centre, but it quickly turned out to have confined the central city to a very small area.

To many, Birmingham had little of architectural distinction to conserve. J. B. Priestley, the author and playwright, visiting the city in 1933, found little to recommend. He stayed at the Grand Hotel on Colmore Row, in his eyes the one and only central city street of much merit, from where he looked down to the Council House (Town Hall) and found 'a sudden access of civic dignity'. But for him, that was it, as unable to escape from 'the sad dingy muddle of factories and dormitories', he complained of 'a parade of mean dinginess'. It was a comment on 'our urban and industrial civilisation'.[6] Contemporary planners, then, inherited both the bleakness characteristic of the industrial heart of Britain in the 1930s and what are now deemed the mistakes of the 1960s. Indeed, despite the postwar prosperity of business, little concern for the environment, in the sense of

Figure 3.3 Birmingham's central shopping area: pedestrianization is spreading as planners try to combat the motor vehicle. *Courtesy of Jon Duffy.*

making it friendly rather than functional, was displayed probably until the 1980s.

Priestley's approbation of Colmore Row doubtless would be repeated if he could revisit today. It has survived to a large degree. But much of the 1960s rebuilding looks already outdated. Birmingham's main railway station in New Street had been replaced by a forlorn underground station which bears no physical bond to the surrounding streets. The old Snow Hill station was finally replaced much later by a nondescript building which has no semblance of being a station to the onlooker. Where visitors to Glasgow, Liverpool, Newcastle and many lesser provincial cities, arrive at grand Victorian railway stations, the gateway to Birmingham is unprepossessing. Plans have been drawn up for another rebuild, but will depend on private finance being forthcoming.

There are other buildings which, retrospectively at least, the planners might have retained: the Victorian central library for one, whose destruction went ahead in the face of vigorous opposition from residents. By the time the city planners had completed their dramatic postwar renewal, comprehensive redevelopment of the type they believed essential was no longer acceptable. Conservation had become the flavour of the time, the environmental orthodoxy. Birmingham, however, was saddled with a concrete box of a centre which it has cost dearly to try and make more human over the last decade.

Yet Birmingham has a key advantage over other provincial cities. It lies in the centre of England, well connected to the rest of the country. Where once it was the hub of the canal system, now it is the motorway which makes Birmingham a convenient location in the late twentieth century: as manufacturing and service industries alike work on leaner and leaner stocks, all the time careful of their financing costs, and increase their reliance on the ability of suppliers to deliver in rapid time, motorway access has become synonymous with economic growth.

Birmingham was the first city linked with London by motorway. A partially elevated expressway (the Aston expressway) was built from the centre to join the motorway at a complex interchange dubbed Spaghetti Junction. New motorways now skirt the south side, another has been added to London by way of Oxford. But the city's competitive location has been undermined by growing congestion just to the north of the interchange. Government plans for relief with an alternative route on the north and eastern side of the conurbation, financed by the private sector and exacting a toll by users, is unlikely to be operational much before the year 2000. Plans for a second orbital route around the western side of the conurbation remained undefined in 1994.

Meanwhile, public transport in Birmingham and its environs has been less well-developed than in London, and even other provincial cities like Manchester and Sheffield, which both now have light-rail networks in place or under construction. Birmingham and the Black Country in 1994 were still waiting for metro plans to gain government financial support. Birmingham Airport, owned by the city council and adjoining local authorities, has been more successful in expansion because it has been able to mix public, including European Union funding, with private finance. It acts mainly as a feeder into continental European cities with a direct service to the United States added in 1993.

In their efforts over the last ten years to counter national perceptions of the city as a concreted and grimy industrial centre, Birmingham's civic leaders have turned to culture. The City of Birmingham Symphony Orchestra, nationally acclaimed and beginning to establish an international reputation, was in 1991 provided with a new symphony hall, complete with advanced accoustics. Public art works were commissioned. One of the two Royal Ballet companies was invited, and accepted, a Birmingham base. D'Oyly Carte Opera Company found a home in the city. The Birmingham Repertory Theatre received a second auditorium. The city council financed refurbishment of the other theatres it owns. All of this was, indeed, 'mobilisation of culture to the cause of city marketing'.[7]

The effectiveness of the public sector-led drive to enhance the environment of the city as a means of drawing investment and jobs from outside depends critically on the response of the private sector. Public initiatives can only set the scene. The national economic recession which hit Birmingham with acute force in the last quarter of 1990 thus emphasized the vulnerability of all the locally inspired efforts at economic development. Although the West Midlands was not affected so severely as the southeast of England in terms of job losses relative to total employment, private-sector investment and consumer confidence were blown severely off course.

The origins of the recession lay in the massive debt accumulated by business and consumers. Interest rates rose to levels which drove most companies to new retrenchment, hastening a process of reorganization which had started with fierce intensity in the early 1980s and continued more slowly during the second half of the 1980s when the regional economy was expanding. Another bout of slimming down by Midlands companies followed, in the same sectors that had been affected in the earlier recession. This time, they were joined by banks, insurance companies and retailers – the new service economy – which were among the hardest hit by the collapse of the housing market. The first casualties of high interest rates, however, were commercial property developers in whose hands rested many of the opportunities for changes to the fabric of the city.

The severity of the blow was evident, for example, in the Council's plans, first, to exploit the site which it had assembled for a mixed commercial development to complement the new convention centre in preparation for a mixed development, and, second, in the reluctance of private finance to come forward for projects in inner city areas earmarked for regeneration.

The 1990s recession proved longer, more severe and given to more false dawns of recovery than the sharp downturn in 1980–1. Recovery in Britain was tempered by the fall in activity in continental Europe, and particularly in Germany. The engineering sector in Birmingham and the West Midlands, which had spent much of the 1980s weaning itself from excessive dependence on the fluctuations of the domestic economy, found itself caught in the very circumstances of weakness its diversification had been designed to avoid. If there was a silver lining, it was that the nature of regional manufacturing, more tied to consumer than capital products, was early into the domestic recession and early out.

It was, in fact, manufacturing which led the West Midlands out of recession. Even before domestic markets strengthened, there was a boost to overseas competitivity from the fall of the value of sterling against the dollar and the currencies closely linked to the Deutschmark following the UK's departure in 1992 from the exchange rate mechanism of the European Monetary System. But this could prove once again to be only a short-term advantage.

3.2 FROM ECONOMIC BOOM THROUGH DECLINE TO A NEW ORDER

The West Midlands grew fast in the 1960s, so much so that it had to endure government-imposed restrictions on industrial companies which wanted to expand locally. Regional planning was in fashion. The government wanted both to disperse industry to the north-east of England, Scotland and Wales, where the economy was less buoyant, and to redistribute people and industry within regions. Birmingham and the Black Country were deemed to need relief not from too little activity, but from too much. Population and industry could be moved to new 'overspill' towns like Redditch and Tamworth, and to Telford in north Shropshire which had hatched the industrial revolution two centuries before. None of the towns grew as fast as the government predicted, but they still proved to be major competitors within the region to Birmingham and the Black Country towns for new investment.

The economic climate changed dramatically when the oil crisis hit the world economy in 1973. It exposed the underlying weakness of British industry – too little investment, poor management and rigid lines of demarcation between unionized trades in the workforce. In the West Midlands, the dominant engineering industry struggled against the superior quality and reliability of continental European manufacturers, particularly those of West Germany. The motor industry in the Midlands – British Leyland, Chrysler – lurched from one crisis to another. The government rescued Chrysler's British operation in the late 1970s, a prelude, as it turned out, of takeover by Peugeot, the French group.

Early in the 1980s, the first Thatcher government launched one more bid to salvage the British-owned sections of the industry. Despite its professed anathema to intervening in the economy, it propped up British Leyland with a big injection of cash in 1981 in preparation for its sale to the private sector. The cars division, by then renamed Rover, went to British Aerospace after the government had paid the group a 'sweetener', part of which it was later required by the European Commission to claw back on the grounds that the deal gave the British company an unfair competitive advantage over other European car makers. British Aerospace sold Rover to BMW, the German car manufacturer, in spring 1994. Jaguar Cars, once part of the old British Leyland, had been privatized earlier, and was bought later by Ford.

British Leyland in all of its guises – cars, vans, four-wheel drive vehicles (Land Rover) – was critically important to the West Midlands. The group had always sourced most of its requirements from British companies, while Ford and General Motors, the Vauxhall manufacturer, had cast their net wider. For the components manufacturers, like Lucas, GKN, Rubery Owen and Automotive Products, all in the Midlands, between 15 and 20% of their turnover came from British Leyland. During the 1980s, however, the group under its new name of Rover built links with Honda, the Japanese manufacturer which bought a minority of the equity. This stimulated an improvement not only in the range of products but in their reliability and the method of their manufacture.

By the early 1990s, Rover had regained commercial credibility. Indeed, it was moving into profit by the time BMW gained control, against a background of political displays of outraged patriotism that a traditional British name should pass into German hands. It was a measure of the changed political climate that Mr John Major's government could applaud the takeover as securing the future of Rover, while Ford's earlier display of interest had been quashed by the Thatcher government on the grounds that the group should remain in British ownership.

The Thatcher government had also gone down another track. It was to woo Japanese car-makers into making Britain their entry point to the European market. Nissan set up, not in the Midlands, but in the north-east of England. It was followed by Honda in Swindon, about 70 miles west of London and Toyota near Derby, in the East Midlands. But all were within reach of the West Midlands and its base of component manufacture. The relatively cheap labour in the region made it particularly attractive to German component makers seeking a low-cost manufacturing base from which to supply what had become the expanding British motor industry.

From 1980 to 1993, 15% of overseas investment into all of the United Kingdom, in terms of employment, went to the West Midlands. So-called foreign direct investment (FDI) was particularly buoyant in Britain as the European Community worked to create, by 1992, a single European market. Nearly half of this investment, however, was made up of expansion by foreign-owned companies already in place. By the mid-1990s, however, other areas of Europe, not least the east, began to look more enticing for companies in search of cheap, compliant and moderately cheap labour. The British place at the head of the list was by no means assured.

The major vehicle components companies in the region have operated globally at least since the early 1980s. The arrival of the Japanese car-makers was one factor which stimulated them into organizing their output to meet more exacting demands for higher quality and 'just-in-time' delivery. They were obliged to forge closer relations with assembly plants and

Conferences and culture

The politicians and representatives of the city's business sector decided to capitalize on the city's geographical position in the centre of England to expand the facilities it could offer to business tourists. The city would build a conference centre. Other cities had done the same, but this would be the best. It was a political gamble, because it called for capital spending which would have to be financed out of the public purse when the policy bias of the central government was to tighten its grip on local authorities and control their spending more rigorously. But there was no party political division about the services sector strategy: indeed, the decision to build a conference centre was taken by a council under Conservative control and brought to fruition by a council under Labour control.

Political control of the city seesawed between the main parties, roughly in cycles of ten years, but the main characteristic of local politics traditionally has been a moderate pragmatism. Retrospectively, this has given the city strength in its dealings with central government, and contrasted with the antipathy which marked the relations of more radical Labour-controlled city authorities in London for much of the 1980s.

Local politicians in Birmingham, whatever their political persuasion, generally could work with business when it was necessary. The Chamber of Commerce had been particularly supportive of economic development plans. This unofficial understanding worked increasingly in the city's favour as partnership between public authorities and the business sector became a pressing requirement of central government. The business community in Birmingham is reasonably small and coherent. A handful of leading businessmen – there are few women in top managerial jobs – appear somewhere on most civic committees. In the past, the link may have been more discreet, according to one of the inner circle. 'It was business which actually ran the city, not the politicians. It was not done openly. The way it worked was that businessmen just let it be known whether they would let something go ahead.'

The physical groundwork for the new conference centre was prepared while the financial plans were also being worked out. The success of the National Exhibition Centre, built just outside the city in the 1970s, provided the confidence and financial guarantee that allowed the new project to go ahead. The quick financial success of the Exhibition Centre surprised many who presumed that London was the only city big enough to stage national and international exhibitions and entertainments. The proposed conference centre, grandly named International Convention Centre, adjacent to the city's main business district, was a larger risk. A new, luxury hotel to be run by Hyatt Corporation, in which the city council would take a financial stake and provide the land, was deemed a necessary adjunct. By the time the Convention Centre and its incorporated Symphony Hall opened in 1991, the cost had soared to £171m.

The logic of such a costly development, even if a quarter of the original budget came from the European Regional Development Fund, could be and was questioned in the knowledge that the complex will be in financial deficit for many years. The City Council, however, never expected that the Convention Centre would be more than, at best, self-supporting; the question, rather, was to estimate what effect the development would have on the wider local economy. Measured against the wider objective of what might be expected from a flagship development, the Convention Centre, notwithstanding its brief history, would seem to have worked. One exhaustive and independent study concluded that it has had 'a pivotal role in revitalizing: the area; confidence among majority of the population; confidence amongst inward investors, especially arts- and office-based activities'.[10]

In architectural terms, it did not score highly, drawing more criticism than praise in the press and publications. Prince Charles registered his disapproval before it was finished. Except for the technically sophisticated interior of the Symphony Hall, the opportunity for Birmingham to redeem its poor reputation in design had not been seized. The point made by Sir Colin Buchanan, author of the 1960s report *Traffic in Towns*, was once again brought home:

> as a nation, we are terribly bad at architecture and civic design . . .
> examples of contemporary architecture at its best . . . are a drop in
> the ocean compared with the vast mass of development.[11]

However, Birmingham enhanced its reputation with the sponsorship of contemporary public art. During the planning for the refurbishment of the city centre, councillors had been persuaded of the possibilities of making the centre more individual, more idiosyncratic, by commissioning artworks.

The conversion of Birmingham's Labour-led council to the use of culture in changing the city's grimy image aroused sharp comment and accusations of waste. And so the 'disconcertingly lumpish Convention Centre was enhanced by engraved glass screens, lighted outlines of coloured birds ever on the move over the entrance, and, wrapped around the internal walls of Symphony Hall, a huge internal mural makes it look as though the building has been turned inside out. The artworks sit rather uncomfortably with the more mundane decor of the conference halls. The central throughway which leads on to a canal bank is open to the public, creating popular space in the conference centre part of the building which is obviously given over to private functions. The centre itself opens on to the most felicitous aspect of the venture . . . a richly patterned pavement in coloured brick'.[12]

Figure 3.6 Raymond Mason's sculpture in a new Birmingham square is called Forward; the city has tried to buy popularity with culture. *Courtesy of Jon Duffy.*

This is Centenary Square, not the least of whose advantages is its success in demonstrating that the planners had at last broken with a policy showing heartless disregard for the pedestrian, while helping to link the central business district with the Edgbaston office centre. Sculptures in this square, and the rebuilt Victoria Square nearby, completed in 1993, were paid for with the aid of the 'Per Cent For Arts' scheme, an undertaking that 1% of building costs of any particular project would be devoted to public arts. The new Symphony Hall, designed to house the City of Birmingham Symphony Orchestra, which was enjoying a wave of critical admiration under its young conductor, Simon Rattle, won universal approbation. Birmingham was being talked about.

> The transformation in barely a few years of Birmingham's image from cultural wasteland to England's most dynamic concentration of cultural activity outside London is a remarkable story of local authority commitment and imagination.[13]

Just how much impact this 'transformation' has had on corporate relocation decision-makers is not yet clear. The Trustee Savings Bank is the only large operation to move into the centre of the city, where it has located its retail banking head office. With much encouragement from the council, it picked a site in the centre of Birmingham for a new building constructed behind a restored nineteenth century façade in Victoria Square. British Gas consolidated its consumer gas division in purpose-built offices in the business park just outside the city boundaries. Otherwise, recent movements have mostly involved the corporate and professional sector which was already in the city.

Some of the city's professional firms have expanded into new offices in the centre, as has Wesleyan Insurance, a Birmingham company. By contrast, Britannic Assurance, another Birmingham company, will move out beyond the city from its present suburban site. Lucas Industries closed its rambling old building in the early 1990s, moved to the suburbs, and sold the site to the City, which started redevelopment with the help of central government finance channelled through the City Challenge, a competitive programme where local private–public sector partnerships bid for funds to concentrate on redevelopment of a narrow geographical area.

Bricks and mortar

In property terms, Birmingham comprises a small central business district, hemmed in by the inner ring road, although this constraint is increasingly being eased by measures to make the road less dominant. Much of the office development in the 1960s took place about one mile west of the centre, in the Edgbaston area. Many of these buildings fall below the comfort and design standards which business came to expect in the 1980s and 1990s. They are out of date in terms of energy conservation, and facilities for accommodating office technologies. Birmingham also has areas on the fringe of the centre which have been given a new lease of life in the last ten years. But the rate of progress is painfully slow by comparison with other cities in Britain and continental Europe. Sites await buyers and action by developers to take up their options.

One of Birmingham's prime sites was created by the Convention Centre. Separated from it only by a narrow canal, Brindley Place since 1987 has passed through the hands of a series of developers: first Merlin International, then Merlin with Shearwater, followed by Shearwater alone and Rosehaugh, Shearwater's parent. Only in 1993 did Argent Estates start work. Plans for use of the site have changed with the developers, starting with festival marketplace shopping and ending in 1994 as a mixed development involving retail, leisure in the form of an aquarium, offices and housing. The hope from the start was to provide Birmingham with the sort of variety and quality of shopping and entertainment which it has mostly lacked. Initially there is a small speculative development of offices, shops and cafes alongside the canal, to be followed by phases for which tenants have been identified. A square will be the centrepiece. Different

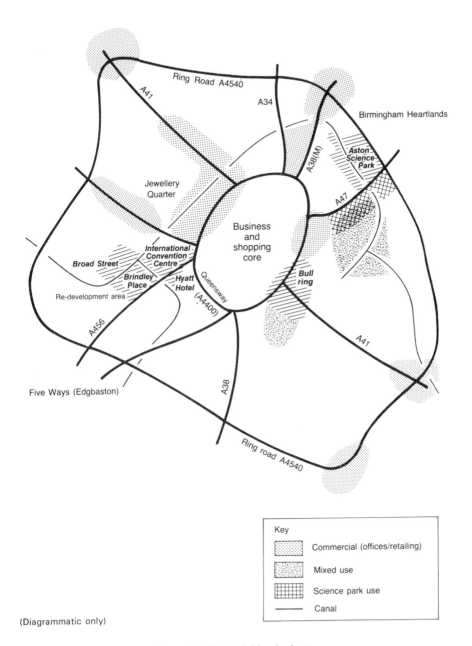

(Diagrammatic only)

Figure 3.7 Central Birmingham.

architects will be employed for the various phases. The key to the success of the much amended scheme will be the quality and cohesion of the whole.

In the mean time, the recession inflicted a serious setback to the planned redevelopment of another part of the city, the 1960s Bull Ring shopping centre. Like the ring roads, it has a very dated appearance, although the rotunda office building is one of the few instantly recognizable symbols of Birmingham. By 1994 there had been five years of discussion on plans for the clearance and redevelopment of the centre. Debate has been angry, punctuated by emotional appeals to preserve the present centre, built where marketplaces have been in existence since the twelfth century. Many poorer people in the city shop in the Bull Ring markets area for essentials. But it had also become dangerously close to ridicule from outsiders who portrayed the 1960s centre as a symbol of the poverty of the city environment.

By the time redevelopment plans had been agreed between the City Council and London & Edinburgh Trust (the owners), and the Council had started the compulsory purchase of properties in the immediate environs, depression on the property market had changed the financial equations. A £500m scheme in a regional city seemed too risky for banks which, in any case, had adopted more stringent lending criteria for property ventures. Notwithstanding the planning considerations which deemed redevelopment an essential part of the upgrading of the city centre, the future of the Bull Ring was highly uncertain in 1994. At best, it would be the end of the decade before it could be completed. More likely, there will be piecemeal improvement to the existing structure.

3.3 BUSINESS SERVICES

Experience during the 1980s suggests that professional firms in the city will resume the expansion which had been suspended by the 1990s recession. The cost structure in Birmingham for services like commercial law is considerably lower than in London. The big accountancy and consultancy firms are firmly established in the city. Business services and professional advice have been successfully 're-defined and re-positioned'.[14] Hopes that banking and finance activities would cluster into a second financial centre outside London have not been realized. Some foreign banks, most serving the ethnic minority population, have opened and Birmingham has a handful of share-dealing firms.

Arguably there is a limit to this expansion. The UK is a small country which leans heavily in the direction of London for government, finance, entertainment and the varieties of professional expertise which combine to form a vibrant services economy. Provincial cities have never been able seriously to challenge the dominance of London. Even in non-financial services, like product design, management consultancy, market research, London and the South East region are dominant. Birmingham actually has more corporate head offices than any British city outside London. But this does not mean that they use the local business services to the exclusion of those provided in the capital.

Birmingham is only 100 miles from London. This can be an advantage over more distantly located centres, since personal contacts in the capital can be so easily sustained. But for local services to be preferred over those offered in the capital, they must be comparable and cheaper at the same time. Companies based in the region tend to use the city for their basic services but turn to London for more specialized advice like merchant banking.

Birmingham's potential expansion in the financial services sector is unlikely to be in the accumulation of head office functions. It is more likely to attract the supporting administrative functions of back offices, where the status of communications and possibilities for the relay of information will be as much determining factors in the choice location as labour and accommodation costs. Telecommunications in Britain was privatized in the 1980s, and a competitor, Mercury Communications, set up, giving the country one of the more price competitive networks within Europe. To this has been added a band of cable companies, many backed by American finance, which have been installing cable for business and entertainment relay. Birmingham Cable Company has invested extensively in switching systems which will mean that subscribers have a greater degree of control over costs of communications within the network area.

3.4 PUBLIC FACE AND PRIVATE PERSONA

Birmingham's appearance has changed much less than the make-up of its people. In this sense, it is a very different city from that of 20 years ago, with extensive change in the age and family structure and in ethnic composition.

The 1991 census figures revealed the extent of the changes for the first time; there had been 'a huge substitution . . . the white, young, economically active had gone'[15] A total of 63 200 workers left the city between 1981 and 1991. 'The majority of these were under 35 and were probably those with skills, qualifications and the dynamism to seek and obtain work in the expanding labour markets elsewhere in the country.'[16] In the same period, over 13 000 workers had dropped out of the labour market altogether, presumably discouraged by the poor prospects of obtaining work. Unemployment was actually slightly lower numerically in 1991 than 1981 – both were recession years – although the rate of jobless was higher

Table 3.2 Ethnic composition of Birmingham, 1991

Ethic background	Percentage
White ethnic group	78.4
Black ethnic group	5.9
Indian, Pakistani, Bangladeshi	14.1
Chinese ethnic group	0.3
Other ethnic groups	1.3

Source: Census, 1991.

in 1991 at 16.2%, a full percentage point above 1981. The economically active population dropped from 541 000 in 1971 to 474 000 in 1981 and thence to 439 000 in 1991. The census recorded 20 000 single parents in the city, of whom 60% do not work.

Birmingham also, on average, has one of the poorest populations in the country. The city ranked fifth in a deprivation table prepared for the government's environment department in 1994, taking into account factors which included unemployment, proportion of children living in low income households, overcrowded households, educational participation rates for 17-year-olds, mortality rate, and the amount of derelict land. Four inner-city London boroughs had a higher poverty index than Birmingham. Liverpool, commonly perceived as the poorest city in Britain, was actually slightly better off than Birmingham. One other West Midlands borough – Sandwell, in the Black Country – came within the unfortunate top ten.

Ethnically, Birmingham is much more mixed than a generation ago. It has one of the country's largest communities of south Asian origin, 14.1% of the city's population. Of these, Pakistani residents are the largest single group, followed by people from India and Bangladesh. The Caribbean community makes up 4.7%. There is a very small Chinese community. Ethnic minority background does not necessarily equate with economic deprivation: the Sikh community, for instance, tends to be well-placed in business. Birmingham has a formal group, the Federation of Asian Business, which is attached to the Chamber of Commerce. By contrast, Bangladeshis and some of the mostly Moslem Pakistanis have a poor command of English and must earn a living, if they can, running a small shop or restaurant.

Tension in the ethnic community tends to be within families, particularly among young people who do not share their parents' feeling of religious and racial exclusivity. With one exception, it has not pervaded the city as a whole. The exception was the Handsworth district, which has a mixed Caribbean and Asian population, the scene for riots and looting by young men in 1982 and 1985. The district, with Toxteth in Liverpool and

Brixton in London, became a byword for racial tension. But government and City funds were diverted to the area for economic development and policing became more sensitive. It would be rash to predict that Birmingham will not suffer more outbursts. Muslim fundamentalism holds an uncertain tension. But race counsellors believe Birmingham's long experience of immigration bodes reasonably well for the future.

Indicators of poverty, or disadvantage, score highest in the inner city and in the municipally owned housing estates on the edge of the city. Some of these districts correlate with a high proportion of ethnic residents. Sparkbrook, once a middle-class residential suburb, still reflected in the old, mostly privately owned and rented housing, but now dominantly Asian in character, has the highest rate of unemployment in the city. Other districts of disadvantage have small numbers from the ethnic minorities: Castle Vale, one of the last and the biggest housing municipal estates built in the city, its towers clearly visible to motorists going through the city on the M6, was prised out of city council control by the lure of special government funding supervised by a government-appointed Housing Action Trust.

Many of the tower blocks of flats constructed during the 1960s in the inner city have been demolished. Others have been renovated with the help of dedicated finance from central government. But much of the public low-rise housing, and private housing, is in equal need of attention. Birmingham introduced an imaginative housing renovation programme in the 1980s which paid owners for the exterior to be rehabilitated as encouragement for them to carry out internal refurbishment – 'enveloping' – but government funding was later withdrawn.

Public authorities – central and local – have tried latterly to target regeneration programmes more on those most in need. In striving to revitalize the Birmingham economy – which is not something, obviously, that a council can do in isolation – the city has an even greater task to see that its strategy gives more chances to the high proportion of disadvantaged. This was the stance that was being stressed by the more left-leaning Labour group that took control of the Council in 1993. It signalled an end to the era of investment in flagship developments. There was even an early run-in for the new leadership on the cost of maintaining the city's cultural icons, in this instance, the symphony orchestra. The necessary support was made available after the highly public staging of a debate which pitted the goal of 'the international city' and culture against the needs of the disadvantaged.

Measured by its budget, Birmingham is the biggest local authority in Britain. Central government transfers funds to the city which amount to a litte less than half of the budget. The balance is raised from residents, through the council tax, a property-based tax which replaced the disastrous community charge, or poll tax, levied on persons but without regard to income, introduced by the Thatcher government; from property taxes paid by business; and from income accruing from the city's extensive property portfolio, including the National Exhibition Centre.

Yet this does not spell freedom for the City Council to act as it wishes. Central government control over local government day-to-day and capital spending has been progressively tightened in recent years since the Thatcher government came to power in 1979. The two-tier government of the big urban areas of England was dismantled in 1986, giving much more responsibility back initially to the single-tier authorities like Birmingham. What followed was the reduction of local control over finance as central government placed limits on the amount which could be raised by local taxation and the removal of functions which traditionally had been held by local authorities. Further education colleges are now funded through bodies appointed by government. Individual schools' governing boards have been given greater policy powers signalling more local control, but are dependent on centrally controlled funding.

This direction of policy had already been foreshadowed in plans to regenerate the big cities – generally lumped together as 'inner city policy' – from 1983 onwards. Areas in urgent need of physical renewal were taken out of the hands of local authorities and placed in the hands of urban development corporations financed directly by central government and given statutory planning powers, on the premise that local government had shown itself unable to do the job itself. Running through all of the policy considerations was the theme that entrepreneurialism was desirable, and that dependency on state benefits was not. The government was convinced that a more dynamic economy in the cities would have to come from the self-starters in business, not through the bureaucrats in town halls.

Economic regeneration programmes dwarfed the dwindling resources of the Urban Programme which had attempted to address the social needs of cities. '. . . if we remove the (private sector-led) economic regeneration strategy, the government does not have an inner city policy'.[17] It became clear, from independent studies, and investigations by the National Audit Office, the parliamentary watchdog over government expenditure, and research commissioned by the government itself, that policies which concentrated on property renewal and entrepreneurial business-type solutions were having little impact on the most run-down areas.

The government then devised the City Challenge programme targeted at neighbourhoods which attempt to combine economic development with measures to strengthen the resources of communities. Local government was brought back into the arena, to help put together partnerships between business and residents in these areas to compete for funds. About two-thirds of the cities and towns long designated by government for special aid succeeded in qualifying for the new programme.

The size and extent of Birmingham's social and economic problems determined that it was at the cutting edge of most government schemes. It was one of the group of inner city partnership authorities which qualified for special funds distributed to schemes which were assessed jointly by central and local government. By 1993, partnerships between public and private sector were required in virtually every regenerative activity which depended on central government finance. Birmingham was also particularly successful in winning finance from the European Regional Development Fund in Brussels – £260m in the ten years to 1994 – which would have been impossible without the backing of the appropriate department of government in London. The Convention Centre, for example, attracted £40m from the European Community.

3.5 HEARTLANDS IN SEARCH OF NEW BLOOD

Birmingham Heartlands to the east of the city centre is an area of 2470 acres in and around the crook formed by the M6 motorway, and the expressway which links the motorway with the city.

The area is typical of many in Britain. Once littered with factories and

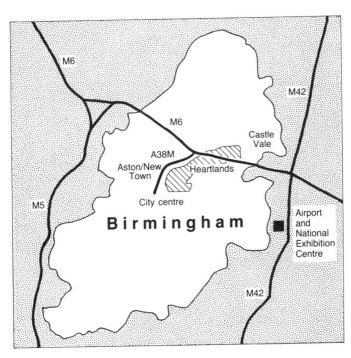

Figure 3.8 Location of Birmingham Heartlands.

housing, it is criss-crossed by the communications of the past – roads, railway lines, canals – but these do not give the fast access to the motorway network which is needed today. The land had been used for a variety of industrial purposes and now bears the legacy in the form of contamination. Redevelopment of the major site in the area is hindered by the presence of live electricity cables. The public sector has subsidized clearance of such sites in the past. The formerly state-owned electricity generating company, now partly private, which owns the site, will want the property market to recover before it decides to act. On other sites, original users have long since departed, or closed down, and the removal of toxic substances, and acquisition of the land for resale lies with the public sector.

Industry and housing lie close together in the casual patterns of the past. Heartlands today has less than 10 000 people. The population fell 20–25% even in the last ten years. Since the clearance of slum dwellings in the 1950s, housing is predominantly publicly owned, much of it in tower blocks. Building high then was assumed to be the best way to conserve some of the high density of slum housing. Low-rise building was introduced later, but this did not stop the rapid physical and social deterioration on the estates.

For all the drawbacks of the slums, they had community. 'The street and its extensions had been the pivot of working-class life in Birmingham's poorer neighbourhoods. . . . But its significance went unrealized until too late, street life fell victim to redevelopment.'[18]

In the last decade, central and local government got together to stop the decay. Public housing has been extensively renovated. One block was turned into residences for old people. Security systems are an integral part of improvement programmes. New social housing – which is built in Britain with the aid of subsidy channelled by the government through the Housing Corporation – is under construction, in accordance with government policy to mix public housing with private and social housing. And now the private sector is coming in.

The showpiece of Heartlands is a small area of new, modestly priced private housing, and social housing, in the area of Bordesley which has succeeded in bringing families back to the area. The target is 1000 new homes, which will support a 'village' with shops and community facilities.

East Birmingham lost large slices of its basic economy from the 1970s onwards. Between 1971 and 1981 4500 jobs disappeared, and a further 5900 in the four years to 1985. By the late 1980s, it had 18 000 jobs, filled predominantly by people living outside the area. The next recession meant more retrenchment. Companies closed down, or moved out of the area, sometimes because of too little space, while other companies in fact have surplus space. Some medium-sized employers remain, including Jaguar Cars, GEC-Alsthom-owned Metro-Cammell, and LDV, formerly Leyland

Daf Vans, which was bought by managers in 1993 to prevent it being closed in the aftermath of financial difficulties in the Dutch parent company. The former Dunlop tyre-making business is still in business as SP Tyres, in Japanese ownership, behind one of the few handsome buildings in the area, Fort Dunlop, which was a storage depot and awaits restoration by its new owners, probably as a factory outlet shopping centre.

A myriad of smaller businesses, often environmentally unattractive, include scrap metal and waste paper processing, container stores, and paint production. No major investment had come into the area. Inner city districts face stiff competition from other towns in their region, in this case, Telford and Tamworth, which offer greenfield sites, and Milton Keynes to the south. South-east England was also emerging as a competitor. Instead of exporting jobs, as seemed likely, the recession had turned the most prosperous region in Britain into a strong competitor for relocating companies. Gradually, however, new sectors of employment were emerging in Heartlands, in distribution, wholesaling, and warehouse-type retailing.

Heartlands, in 1988, was the renewal target of a group of contractors and developers and the City Council. They formed a development agency under the control of a company, with modest equity, as an alternative to an urban development corporation, which was what the government had planned for the area. Urban development corporations are financed directly by government, and had been set up in, among other places, east London (London Docklands), Merseyside, the North East, and the Black Country. Most will be wound up by 1997. Core funding from government enables them to buy up land, compulsorily if necessary, and prepare it for sale to the private sector.

The agency model, on the other hand, preserved the local council role in the partnership. And this was also maintained when the agency was wound up, and a development corporation for Heartlands was eventually set up, in 1992. The agency had made a good start in getting offices into the area, and housing, but most development had come to a virtual standstill by 1990 with the rest of the property market in the city. 'For some purposes, the Heartlands model seemed to work very effectively; but the absence of core grant posed problems in addressing major developments . . . especially in recession conditions.'[19]

Road improvements continued, however. Plans to construct the road which will make a big improvement to communications and open up sites for development did not get under way until 1994, however. In the short time available to the development corporation, it may prove too late to revive the property momentum.

In the social arena, Heartlands may be more successful. The area became a test bed for new ideas to help improve the quality of life generally. It had the first business-education Compact in the city. Training was earmarked for several pilot schemes aimed at improving the chances of the local population to get jobs. Community development has also been a constituent of the Heartlands philosophy from the start. Tenant management was introduced by central government in an area of public housing which will be extended to other districts, and other parts of the country.

The challenge spreads

Two districts on either side of Heartlands were subsequently designated for special attention from central government. The programmes are different, however. City Challenge focuses on the area of Newtown with its 1960s public housing much in decline, and the once prosperous commercial sector in south Aston. The Housing Action Trust has been set up on the Castle Vale housing estate on the outskirts of the city boundaries. Both districts need huge injections of capital to prevent further deterioration of the physical structure, and social deprivation. A new shopping complex was the first target for the residents of Newtown. The City Challenge area has 850 businesses, most small, which might form the base for employment growth in the area. Training schemes are high on the agenda. Business start-ups are another focus. Newtown residents, most living in housing owned by the local council, will be given the opportunity to get involved in local government at the district level as part of an experimental scheme agreed between the council and government to devolve a degree of control over services.

The regeneration effort in this area is not wholly government-driven however. Aston is the location for a proposed community development bank which Birmingham Settlement, a long-established voluntary agency in the city, has been trying to set up for many years as a means to halt the departure of business from the area. Early in 1994, the trust which will run the bank was seeking £3.5m initial capital from public and private sources.

The programme of the Housing Action Trust in Castle Vale – similar trusts have been formed in problem housing areas in several cities – takes the management of the housing out of the control of the local council for several years while renovation, and demolition, is undertaken. At the end of the period, residents decide whether they want to go back under council ownership, or go to private landlords, or a housing association.

Each programme depends on effective partnerships being formed between public authorities, and between them and the private sector, and voluntary agencies. Central government, however, demands detailed control over how its money is being spent, which inevitably inhibits more creative solutions to stimulate regeneration. A reorganization of government administration in spring 1994, however, gave more financial flexibility to officials at the level of the regions. Each region was allocated part of the national regeneration budget. The skill of local councils would be in putting together the partnerships which must satisfy government before funds for identified projects would be released. Cities have to compete for this money not only between themselves, however, but also with suburban and rural districts in the region, some of them having good claims for funds to stimulate their economies.

3.6 POLISHING UP THE JEWELLERY QUARTER

The only district of old Birmingham to survive the bulldozer is the one-time hub of the jewellery-makers, goldsmiths and silversmiths. The Jewellery Quarter owes its preservation primarily to the fact that the City Council ran out of money. It had been scheduled for complete redevelopment in the 1960s. The only exception to the policy was St Paul's Square, part of the ward for which Joseph Chamberlain was once elected, with its eighteenth-century church.

The Jewellery Quarter's recent history is a chronicle of the conversion of the planners and the people to the cause of preservation. In 1970 the *Birmingham Post* described the quarter as 'an uninspiring area of crumbling brickwork and decay', while *The Times* pronounced it 'ripe for redevelopment'. By the mid 1970s, protests from around the country had been

Figure 3.9 The Jewellery Quarter in Birmingham: saved from the bulldozer but finding now that refurbishment is painfully slow. *Courtesy of Jon Duffy.*

orchestrated against the redevelopment plans. The district which had been the home of the Birmingham gun-makers had already met death by bulldozer. Then, in 1976, the industrial architecture of the Jewellery Quarter was being praised, described as 'almost unique as a surviving area of small workshops . . . only the Clerkenwell area of London matches the distinctiveness of the Quarter'.[20] A year later, *Country Life* magazine was the surprising sponsor of the area,[21] advocating that it be made a pilot industrial improvement area. The government of the day was looking even then for solutions to what it saw as the inner-city problem. The City Council seemed to like the idea, and put together a scheme along those lines. The plan was that some of the industrial processors would be encouraged to stay, and the jewellery-makers likewise, while new service type business would be encouraged to move in.

The area occupied by the jewellers had not been a beautiful place, although some buildings had some finer points. They had mostly been terraced housing, which was converted into workshops, over which the owner and his family lived. As the owners became wealthier, they moved their homes to the then new suburbs like Handsworth Wood. But some stayed on, in increasingly insanitary conditions, hence the justification for the original redevelopment plan for most of the area.

The district also contained some of the first purpose-built factories, as opposed to mills, which made everything from steel pens and nibs – enough to serve the whole of the British Empire – and more sophisticated items like laboratory equipment. Industry still survives in the area, its origins sometimes in processes close to the original jewellery-makers – electro-plating, and toolmaking, but most have gone, leaving behind buildings which have fallen into disrepair. A few of the remaining Victorian buildings have been restored by small scale developers which concentrate on inner city areas. These provide workshops, offices and studios, usually at fairly modest rents on short-term leases, which encourages small firms in film-making, software design, public relations and architecture. Private housing has also made a cautious debut, or perhaps return would be more accurate.

The revival of the area under its new title of the Jewellery Quarter has been a qualified success. Its location close to the city centre has been the vital ingredient in its becoming a fringe area for offices. Development by the purely private sector has been carried out by local developers, in small bites. Stone-setting and cutting and jewellery-making is still carried on in workshops. Dozens of shops sell cheap jewellery, most of it imported, but the area has not yet become the sort of quarter characteristic of continental European cities, and many former industrial cities in Britain.

Derelict buildings and land which has been vacant sometimes for 20 years are a reminder that owners of inner-city land will hold on indefinitely sometimes in the hope that they will get better prices, but in the process are retarding improvement of the area overall which was the goal.

A recovery in the commercial property market will stimulate some take-up of sites. Demand for private housing in the area has not been decisively established. The planners were opposed to housing in the area for many years, despite the evidence that it is normally the first sector to revive inner-city areas, because of the industry bias of the original plan. When they changed their minds, there were no buyers. The Jewellery Quarter still has a long way to go.

NOTES

1. Jacobs, J. (1968) *The Economy of Cities*; Vintage Books edn, 1970.
2. Ibid.
3. Waller, P. J. (1983) *Town, City and Nation, 1850–1914*, Oxford University Press.
4. Chinn, C. (1989) *Developing Birmingham*, Birmingham City Council.
5. Briggs, A. (1963) *Victorian Cities*, Odhams Press; pbk edn, Penguin Books, 1990.
6. Priestley, J. (1934) *English Journey*, Heinemann; pbk edn, Penguin Books, 1977.
7. Bianchini, F. and Parkinson, M. (eds) (1993) *Cultural Policy and Urban Regeneration*, Manchester University Press.
8. *Residents Voice*, April 1994.
9. *Financial Times*, 21 October 1983.
10. Smyth, H. (1994) *Marketing the City*, E & FN Spon.
11. Buchanan, C. (1975) Cities in crisis: an overview, *The Planner*, July/August.
12. Cork, R. in Fisher, M. and Owen, U. (eds) (1991) *Whose Cities?*, Penguin Books.
13. Lister, D. in Fisher and Owen, *Whose Cities?*, *op. cit.*
14. Roger Taylor, Chief Executive, Birmingham City Council, 1994, in interview with the author.
15. Ibid.
16. *The Birmingham Economy Review and Prospects* (1994) Birmingham City Council/Birmingham Training & Enterprise Council.
17. Deakin, N. and Edwards, J. (1993) *The Enterprise Culture and the Inner City*, Routledge.
18. Chinn, C. (1994) *Homes for People*, Birmingham Books.
19. Deakin and Edwards, *The Enterprise Culture and the Inner City*, *op. cit.*
20. Crawford, A. (1976) *A Walk in the Jewellery Quarter*, Victorian Society.
21. Binney, M. (1977) Struggle for survival, *Country Life*, March.

Rotterdam

4

Figure 4.1 Map of the Netherlands showing the Randstad group of cities.

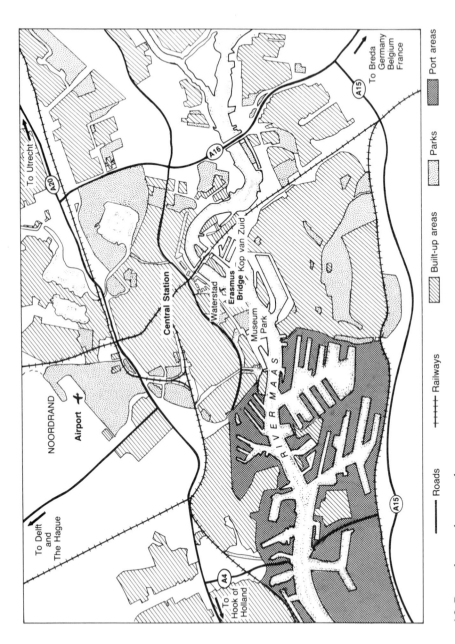

Figure 4.2 Rotterdam and surrounds.

Table 4.1 Basic facts about Rotterdam, 1993

(a) Population (city of Rotterdam):	596 116
(New Rotterdam region)	1 137 776
(b) Ethnic minorities:	19.1%
(c) Percentage of social housing:	57.5%
(d) Employment by sector	

Sector	No. employed
Trade, banking	88 786
Industry	40 827
Construction	13 627
Services	78 048
Public utilities	2 251
Transport	46 298
Port	7 168

(e) Unemployed people	52 500

(f) Top five corporations (by employment)
1. Shell
2. Nedlloyd Shipping
3. Croon Elektrotechniek
4. ICI
5. Rietschoten & Houwens

4.1 INTRODUCTION

Where the river flows down to the sea

Rotterdam symbolizes the struggle of western Europe to achieve world-class status, at a time when the city is coming to terms with more dramatic social, ethnic and economic change than at any time in its 750 years.

Unlike most north European industrial cities, Rotterdam still has a powerful reason for being in existence. From its earliest days this was a port. But it was the nineteenth-century industrialization of Germany, and of Great Britain, that spurred its development. In 1864, work started on an ambitious project, constructing a channel which linked the city docks with the mouth of the River Meuse (Maas) which became the outlet for the Rhine into the North Sea. The channel, finally completed to the required depth 20 years later, was a giant leap forward. It made navigation safer, and meant that the port could handle larger ships. Coming with the construction of new inland waterways to the German industrial hinterland, Rotterdam became the import and export port for Germany's burgeoning iron and steel industry.

The prosperity of the port of Rotterdam still depends on these fundamentals: the health of other European economies, particularly Germany; finding the finance for a rolling programme of investment to upgrade the port's facilities, and the upgrading of the transport channels between port and markets. For 30 years, Rotterdam has proudly topped the world port charts in tonnage handled. In 1993, 280m tonnes went through the port. That was less than in the previous two years, reflecting the downturn in the German economy. But the forecast is that Rotterdam will handle nearly 400m tonnes in 15 years' time, assuming that investment plans to provide more space within the port will be implemented and that European economies maintain competitive positions. The growth of ports serving the Pacific Rim, led by Singapore, is a salutary reminder of the competitive forces in Far East economies.

The strength of Rotterdam – port and people – has always been its ability to adapt in the face of challenge, and, in the past, adversity. Rotterdam in the 1990s plans to make its port much more than an entrepot centred primarily on tonnage throughput. It wants to intensify the process of adding value to the goods handled, and encourage more high value refining of the basic materials which come into the port. Rotterdam has been investing in facilities for handling containerized traffic since the 1950s, when the Europoort was built on land reclaimed from the sea. But more space is needed now within the port area, and improvements must be made to the road and rail arteries from the port to the hinterland to the standard of at least those around Antwerp, its main competitor for container business.

Location confers status

Rotterdam is a small city (596 000) which sits at the southern end of the circle of cities in the western Netherlands that make up the Randstad, whose population totals 6.8 million. The Rotterdam metropolitan area is nearly 1.2 million, which will have its own government in 1997. The growth of the Rotterdam region is pushing it towards convergence with the Hague – the seat of the Dutch national government. The two cities have a combined population of 2.5 million. The Randstad swings down from Amsterdam, though the Hague, Rotterdam and back up to Utrecht. Rotterdam is part of this zone, and also at the tip of the corridor formed by the Rhine and the Schelde rivers, which embraces Antwerp in Belgium, at the top of the Belgian trio of cities of Antwerp, Ghent and Brussels.

Belgium and the Netherlands (with Luxembourg) were in a customs-free zone even before the Treaty of Rome set up the European Economic Community in 1957. Since 1992, the single market, without customs, and stripped of non-tariff barriers, has come into place across the European Union. (The EEC gave way to the European Community, which, since the member states of the Community ratified the Maastricht Treaty, has come to be known as the European Union.)

The flat, low-lying land around Rotterdam, and north Flanders attracted enormous investment by American and European oil and chemical multinationals in the aftermath of World War II making it one of the big industrial regions of western Europe as well as one of the distribution hubs. Within the region, the ports of Rotterdam and Antwerp are competitors. Latterly, both cities have sought more service industries and head offices. Cultural facilties, quality offices and city centres are the means to shed the image of cities which have been seen as industrial appendages of Brussels and Amsterdam.

The Randstad is pivotal to the health of the Dutch economy. The port of Rotterdam, and Amsterdam's Schiphol airport are the key development points. Rotterdam's port and industry contribute over 10% of the gross national product. For every job in the area of the port, it supports another three jobs. The petrochemicals complex is the biggest in the Netherlands, one of the largest in Europe, and a major exporter.

But the concentration on oil-based industries has brought its own problems with the fluctuation of the world oil price, and a heavy toll on the environment. After the recession of 1980–81, Rotterdam renewed its efforts to diversify its economy. The traditional strengths of the urban Randstad have been challenged by the regional led economic regeneration programmes in the former coal mining area of Limburg which has been heavily supported by national and European funds. The employment base of the cities, meanwhile, has been filtering out. 'Within the western Netherlands there has been a shift of economic activity and with it of employment from the cities to surrounding areas, and the region as a whole has fallen back relative to the rest of the country.'[1]

The state stands back

Successive governments have been criticized for failing to invest sufficiently to upgrade the infrastructure in the area. The main highways which carry port traffic suffer from bottlenecks, the siting of the high-speed rail network on which France embarked a generation ago has still to be decided, and good commuter rail links between the cities of the Randstad are lacking. 'If the Randstad is to function as a metropolis, the communications need to be greatly improved in terms of speed and frequency of services.'[2] Business also complained that the pricing of telephone services was high in relation to other countries, and the technology lagging. The first stage towards selling the government-owned posts and telecommunications to the private sector was launched in May 1994. And, after years of lobbying, and deliberation, the go-ahead was given in 1993 for a freight rail line to be built between Rotterdam and the German border, where it will link in with the European freight network, part of a Fl 7 billion package of infrastructure improvements planned for the whole country. The Dutch government wants 20% of the cost of the Betuwe freight line to be financed by transport companies which will use the line.

The European high-speed rail line will offer passenger and freight transport to Belgium, Germany as well as France when it is extended, and to Britain through the Channel Tunnel which was scheduled to come into operation late in 1994. The port expects traffic of goods on the roads will double over the next 15 years, in addition to more freight being sent by rail. These are major considerations in any country, and particularly in the Netherlands, the most densely populated country in Europe. The critics can argue that more roads, and high-speed rail, simply create more traffic and sometimes unnecessary journeys, which quickly cancel out the benefits of investment.

Speeding up the decision-making

The need to speed up the process of getting major projects off the ground is one of the reasons put forward for the new government of the metropolitan area which will come into being in 1997. The council will be set up to merge Rotterdam with 18 other municipalities in the area. The present higher tier of government in the area will be abolished. Rotterdam meanwhile will break up into 10 districts, each with a council, for local functions. The functions of the new 'stadsregio Rotterdam' are still being sorted out, but the plan must include strategic land-use planning. For example, the City Plan of Rotterdam calls for 65 000 new dwellings, 15–20 000 of them within Rotterdam, to be provided over the next 20 years. The new body can be expected to ask the lower tier authorities to identify land banks for development purposes. Education, economic development, will be likely to go to the higher authority.

The new arrangement for government has not been forced upon Rotterdam. In fact, its council was a prime mover in getting central government to effect the reorganization. Regional government is also scheduled for other parts of the country. The reasoning behind Rotterdam's lobbying was that the city as currently structured is too small to implement major development plans, in addition to infrastructure, like the Kop van Zuid, and the proposed new airport and associated development plan.

Rotterdam, and other Dutch cities, can only modernize with the support of the state. Big capital projects obviously depend on central government's priorities. The Netherlands system of government is highly centralized, and local government is closely regulated, although Rotterdam has slightly more financial leeway since it gets an income from its port and land holdings. Local politicians have hopes that the new regional council will be given a greater degree of flexibility than is the case now. The high dependency of local administration on central government support also means that there is less urgency to work with the business community than under systems where the finance of the local council depends to a larger extent on business property taxes.

Dutch economic policy is hedged about by the budget deficit, which amounted to 3.9% of net national income in 1993, and the commitment to maintain the value of the Dutch guilder within close range of the German Deutschemark. These are tough goals, not only deemed necessary by politicians in purely practical terms, but also because the Netherlands has been a leading advocate of the European countries moving towards monetary union, which, in principle, will mean a common currency and harmonization of tax regimes between the EU members. The push to cut the national budgetary deficit has meant a reappraisal of subsidized projects in the cities, particularly urban renewal, where Rotterdam still has a huge programme to complete.

Spending constraints have also caused the Dutch to re-examine their social support which is one of the most comprehensive in Europe. The rise in the number of unemployed in the country following the fall-out in industry pushed up the benefits bill, as well as hitting cities particularly hard. In the last budget in autumn 1993 of the coalition government that was voted out in spring 1994, it became more difficult for individuals to qualify for unemployment benefit, as an example. But this was linked to a package of measures to encourage job creation. They included a cut in the minimum wage, new tax abatement measures to encourage expansion by small firms, and increased investment in research and development. There was 'something to be said for the fundamental rethink the government has triggered about the role of the welfare state'.[3]

Dutch workers and trade unions have maintained a stronger presence in the organization of the labour force than in the United States and Britain. They have been reluctant to move towards the sort of work practices, like part-time working and contract employment, that have helped to reduce the unemployment rates, and pleased employers anxious to benefit from more flexibilities in pay and working hours, for instance, and in the roles performed by employees.

The sophisticated city search

Politicians and employers in Rotterdam have juggled with maintaining a competitively costed economy within a tradition of a socially responsible system of local government. But the city has been unable to shake off the effects of the adjustment of Europe to the rigours of the international economy which followed the prosperity of the immediate postwar years. The ramifications of recession gave rise to a new episode in the renewal of the city districts which has been ongoing since 1945. After the decade of doing up the old districts, the socialist-leaning city government gave way to a more moderate coalition. A new generation of planners began thinking about Rotterdam as an international city. 'We were looking for a sort of renewal of urban renewal.'[4]

Of course, Rotterdam always had an international perspective. As the site of the major port in a nation which is highly dependent on trade, it could not possibly look inwards. If you stop anybody in the centre of Rotterdam, it is very likely that they have a very good command of another language than Dutch. It has the head offices of Unilever, Anglo-Dutch food processing group, and of shipping companies, Nedlloyd Shipping, Smit, Pakhoed Transport & Storage, as well as Robeco investment group and ING-Bank.

But Rotterdam has not yet come to vie with London, Paris, Geneva, Brussels and Frankfurt, as does neighbouring Amsterdam, for the head offices of multinational corporations. Rotterdam was a working man's city with few cultural and recreational facilities, and very little choice in housing type or tenure. To change the reality, and the image, was the task that the urban planners set themselves in the mid 1980s.

> It is not only factors such as accessibility, nearness of supply routes and markets, and attractive conditions for establishing a business that are considered essential . . . The industrial [world] cities will have to revalue their human and cultural resources as well as their self-constructed environment. They must be in a position to offer future intellectuals a 'quality of life' and a stimulating working environment which can compete with that of other world cities.[5]

Plans for physical and cultural renewal are being realized in the Waterstad, with new museums, restoration of the remaining bits of old Rotterdam, and the emergence of the first fruits of public-sector-assisted investment in the Wilhelminapier area of the south bank, and luxury apartments. It would not be churlish, however, to realize that Rotterdam is doing what many industrial cities in North America and Europe have been doing, and that these are moves that might, but only might, pin down mobile international investment.

The way in which this radical change in the policy direction of the city was shaped owed much to a 'technocratic-elitist mode of operating in Rotterdam',[6] which is unusual in Dutch cities. The style of policy-making seemed to have evolved from an informal coalition of individuals, bureaucrats, financiers and community leaders, whose ideas were backed by the elected mayor and aldermen, who form the working executive wing of the council.

This sort of consensus between public and private figures is not the norm in the Netherlands.

There is still no easy, flexible and direct interaction between the business sector and local government in the metropolitan areas. Such an interaction . . . demands a Dutch equivalent of the 'civic culture', the local concern and pride, found in North America. Such a concern with one's own locality automatically produces the necessary linkages and strategic coalitions essential to economic and infrastructural development.[7]

People characteristics

But renewal had to be about people as well as buildings. Rotterdam, as in many cities in Europe, is coping with racial, social as well as economic change. Those changes are reflected in a population which is increasingly dependent on the state for its livelihood. Of 52 500 people registered as unemployed, over 20% of the working age population, nearly 30 000 have been out of work for a year or more. There is more than a suspicion among the people who are in work that some of those out of a job do not want one in any case. There is a threat that young people who go on refusing jobs will have their benefits cut off. Immigrants make up about 35% of registered unemployed in the city, against 19% of the population.

The first migrants to the city came in the 1960s from the Mediterranean, and they came to work in the shipyards. They were succeeded by people from the former Dutch colonies, particularly Surinam, and they were joined by migrants from Turkey, Morocco, and many other countries. Rotterdam boasts about 38 nationalities among its population. Forty per cent of children up to the age of 14 have an ethnic minority background. They have tended to settle in the older districts of the city where some 'black' schools have as many as 80% from ethnic minorities. The multiplicity of backgrounds and languages makes the teaching task in these schools very demanding. Government policy is to get immigrants to speak Dutch, so enabling them to integrate. Separate ethnic development is not encouraged. But critics say that the government has not delivered sufficient financial backing to see language tuition reach its goal.

Rotterdam does not have real poverty because the state benefit system is generous enough to provide a sound floor. But it has most of the social ills of cities, if not always to the degree of cities which demonstrate deep class divisions. So it has drug-related crime, vandalism and football hooliganism, which can be crimes. There is lots of graffiti around, the police say middle-class youth is mainly responsible. The Dutch also have a legendary liberal attitude to drugs. Visitors to Rotterdam are surprised to see an open-air compound next to the central station where addicts can meet with each other, and volunteers from churches and groups trying to help them.

The new society which has taken hold in Rotterdam threatens to introduce a class differential which has not been present in the city. Rather than let it happen, there has been an attempt to encourage people to take more control over their lives and their neighbourhoods. Social Innovation is a sort of renewal among people which happens to fit in with the authorities' desire to get people off social benefits. Social Innovation's aim was to help people to help themselves more, as individuals, as parents, as workers, as residents in the neighbourhood. This peculiarly Dutch programme has provided one of the most interesting episodes in Rotterdam social history, – it has now been adopted in other cities in the Netherlands. The programme was a sort of pilot which has been subsumed into the network of community groups and public agencies. Its demise was deliberate, since its architects did not want it to grow into a bureaucracy of its own.

Getting people into work is the main objective of government. One quarter of school-leavers have no qualifications. Rotterdam does not have the network of partnerships between business and schools. The assumption is that the state does what it is good at, and business gets on with its life. Rotterdam is experimenting with a Compact which concentrates on students taking vocational training courses who are in danger of failing to complete their course. Students, parents, the training institute, and employer all become parties to a contract which guarantees the student a job or further course of training with the partner company once the certificate has been earned.

The impetus in Rotterdam to change things has come mostly from the public side. But there is growing evidence that the electorate, and business, believes itself to be out of harmony with the politicians, and the politicians to be weary, without ideas, in contrast to the active second half of the 1980s. The coalition government, elected in Spring 1994, will spend much of its time preparing for the reorganization of government.

4.2 LAND-USE PLANNING

Making the most of everybody's land

In the mid 1980s, a new city council set about enticing property developers to come back to Rotterdam. The developers had all but turned their backs on Rotterdam where the City Council's extensive land holdings gave it the ability to call the tune, and it had not encouraged new development for some time. The heart of the oldest bit of the port in the city, with its web of inland waterways and close proximity to the centre, was an obvious starting point. The city put up the Maritime museum and the Inland Shipping Museum, and the IMAX theatre-cinema, in a bid to create interest. Housing construction in modest proportions got going, and a hotel and offices. Public money accounted for the lion's share of investment in this area, known as the Waterstad.

Land-use planning in Rotterdam is largely the product of the twentieth century. Little thought was given by the city fathers to the lay-out of the city prior to that, although there was always a particular discipline needed in coping with the system of dikes which still dictate the physical lay-out of the city. Government became forced to intervene, however, when infectious diseases became rampant in the rapidly industrializing nineteenth-century city. The canals built to take the waste from the old city became breeding grounds of cholera until a drainage and pumping system was installed, which permitted waste to be transported from canals to the river. But disease returned, this time to the overcrowded dwellings by now crammed on to the south bank of the river. The area had been opened up in 1878 with the construction of a bridge, and rapidly became home to thousands who moved to Rotterdam to work in the port. By the end of the century, the municipality had set up proper supplies of water, and planned for the removal of sewage, and provision of essential services.

Decent housing then became the city's top priority. The legal authority for provision to be made for housing was given in the 1901 Housing Act. This was the legislation which opened the way for charitable (not for profit) housing associations to control a large part of the city's housing. However, a part of Rotterdam's housing was still in the hands of private landlords. Maintenance of these properties was minimal. Then, in May 1940, the German bombardment of the centre of the city flattened 25 000 houses in the historic city triangle. Workshops and factories disappeared. So did a hundred public buildings. The death toll was over 1000, and 78 000 Rotterdammers were homeless.

Very early on after this disaster, plans were being made for the rebuilding of Rotterdam. But, after the war, the politicians scrapped these plans and seized on the opportunity to solve some of the traffic problems that had clogged up the old city when it was still there. Virtually nothing of the old city remains today. What had not been bombed was bulldozed. 'Everything still standing – there's a list of 114 properties, some of them architectural showpieces, which could have been saved – was torn down and carried off as rubble'.[8] The city architect took the opportunity to plan a city which would be fit for the age of the car.

The city centre that emerged was functional but drab, and it died after six o'clock at night, in contrast to the old city. 'What were meant to be boulevards in the heart of the city became motorways. The town was actually bleeding dry.'[9] To some critics, the shape of the centre simply reflected the priorities that had always dictated the shape of Rotterdam. The government had made the docks, damaged extensively towards the end of World War II, the first priority for reconstruction and the city centre was to be re-built strictly as a commercial centre.

> Building the city has always come at the bottom of the list (after the harbour) which has resulted in a patchwork quilt. After the destruction of the World War II, the same thing happened again. Repairing the harbours had priority, in order to get the Dutch economy on its feet again. To a great extent the city went by the board, and despite grandiose plans was helped along from one one-off project to the next.[10]

The new Willems bridge was an example:

> an imposing span which would lead one to expect a magnificent connection between the two parts of the city on either side of the Maas, but in fact has barriers at both ends rather than logical connections.[11]

The historical perspective is necessary in order to appreciate the changes that are being implemented today. The city's post-war reconstruction had put down some architectural markers and imaginative use of space: De Bijenkorf department store in Coolsingel; Churchillplein with its magnificent statue, The Destroyed City, symbolizing the tragedy of wartime destruction; the World Trade Centre; and public housing of designs and standards far superior to most in Europe.

Figure 4.3 Erasmus Bridge is under construction; it will link the city centre to the new 'city on the Maas'. *Courtesy of Cas Schook, Mijnsheerenland, Netherlands.*

The new Rotterdam is not a soaring, head-in-air, aluminium place. She does not blaze with colour and vivacity, like the flamboyant masterpieces of Mexico and Brazil. Nor does she spring frankly from her own mercantile roots, like the new city of London. Au fond she is, I suppose, a Bauhaus city, a square, solid, knife-edged, intensely functional entity. Her new suburbs are endless, handsome expanses of rectangular blocks; her heart is rich and imposing and admirably organized; but she feels queerly unsympathetic.[12]

The 1990s is seeing a renewed emphasis on architecture. The new Erasmus Bridge signals 'the new emphasis on quality after the emphasis on quantity. It marks the point of no return for the whole city.'[13] The mid-1980s can be seen now as the watershed in Rotterdam's postwar planning history, from the period dominated by the need to replace and provide, to that of a city preparing to preen itself before the critical eyes of the world.

Homes for all

Housing has an emotive ring for Rotterdammers which reflects a recognition of the awful conditions of the past, exacerbated by the severe accommodation shortages post World War II in most Dutch cities, and many other European cities – because of bombing, but also because of the urgent need to rehouse people out of slums. In the Randstad the problem was particularly acute. It took until 1960 for Rotterdam to replace all of the housing that it had lost in 1940; in the city itself and in the new towns which were built in the suburbs. But the population had risen, buoyed by the birth rate and workers flooding into the port that was burgeoning on the back of the German economic recovery.

In 1965, there were 732 000 Rotterdammers. As it turned out, it was the peak. But accommodation in general, and single family homes in particular, were still in short supply. By the 1970s, the postwar 'baby boomers' were also beginning to want their own homes. From the 1960s, families were streaming out of the industrial city to the greener suburbs. The natural direction of past development of the city along the river now shifted to the north and the east. Some of the new centres were identified deliberately by the planners to take out-of-town offices, which meant public transport connections were essential. The municipal housing built in the 1960s on the outer periphery is now urgently in need of repair and improvement.

Better-off families went for single units and were much more likely to buy their homes. A substantial element of the suburban seekers in the Randstad were 'higher-status populations . . . and these classes may even predominate in such movement such that the pauperization of the centre results'.[14] Over 40% of the housing that was being built in the suburbs was for owner occupation. The effect on the city was devastating. In 1971 there had been 116 000 families with children in the city; by 1989 the number was down to 85 500, and 26 200 of these families were headed by a single parent.

Nor did Rotterdam experience the 'embourgeoisement' of its older districts, as was common in North America and Europe in the 1960s and 1970s. Rotterdam's population decline had started in the 1970s, and the city went on to suffer a net loss of people at the rate of 15 000 a year in that decade. The urban renewal programme was under way in the older districts and immigrants were replacing the departing white families. The rise in immigration almost certainly accelerated the exodus to the suburbs. 'Urban renewal did many things for Rotterdam but it did nothing to stop the middle classes leaving the city.'[15]

New homes for old

Rotterdammers got tired of the pulling down period that had characterized the changing city. The old districts in the inner city became the focal point of dissent, with demonstrating residents and small business owners, seeing their livelihoods threatened, deciding to march to the town hall. One district in particular, which had been set aside for new buildings for the university, aroused passionate opposition. The tide turned when the government introduced a policy of urban renewal, meaning rehabilitation of old housing, in Rotterdam and other Dutch cities. Eight districts were targeted initially. These dwellings suffered from poor maintenance adding to the fact that they had often been badly built in the first place. Building regulations in Rotterdam had been particularly lax. Meanwhile, the system whereby rents were strictly controlled made improvement an uneconomic proposition for landlords.

The authorities stepped in. The council bought up thousands of properties from landlords, who were offered a bonus of 25% of the market price if they agreed to sell quickly. A long-term programme of renovation followed. The work was carried out street by street so that as far as possible the character of the area would not be destroyed by necessitating a lot of people to move away. In 1979, the city formed a new department, DROS, which was given combined responsibility for physical planning and urban renewal.

Neighbourhood know-how

Project planning groups were set up in the neighbourhoods. The Council appointed the representatives of the residents to these groups, which are charged with drawing up the project plan for their neighbourhood, and

Figure 4.4 Child in a revived suburb: the city wants neighbours to assume more responsibility for their streets. *Courtesy of Rotterdam City Council.*

gave them the opportunity to engage planning advisers at a cost on the public purse. The groups focused mainly on housing matters at first, but later they were able to expand their brief so that the concerns of small businesses and shopkeepers in their area can be taken on board. The other concerns of the community, like the use of drugs and prostitution, or worries about education, are also taken into account, if that is what the groups want.

These community-based groups have coalesced into another organization created by the council which encourages residents to take responsibility for the maintenance and improvement of their neighbourhoods. It retains two important features characteristic of the project groups: the City representatives still have a mandate to make decisions on these relatively minor matters without having to go back to the town hall all of the time; and the representation of the residents in deciding how to look after their neighbourhoods.

The City is now more concerned than in the past with variety as well. They actually want the districts to stay individual. 'We're now looking for the individual identity of an area and seeking to build on that.'[16] And they are bringing in the private sector both to build and to improve existing housing.

New role for housing associations

Housing associations build and manage the sector which is called social housing in the Netherlands. They were designated in the 1901 Housing Act as the only private institutions which could build and manage housing with government support, and were required to plough back any profits into housing. They have a significant presence in Rotterdam, providing housing for 57% of the population of the city. They, like many institutions, are undergoing changes which will make them more private. By the mid 1990s, government subsidies, which account for 40% of some associations' income, will have been phased out. The state's control over the rents that they can charge, however, will be moderated. So will its control over costs. For instance, they will be 'under pressure to pay more for land . . . [But] we can borrow, the guarantee is very secure'.[17] A new housing association is being set up to take over the city's 40 000 subsidized dwellings, which is the largest stock of public housing in the Netherlands.

Housing associations will still be expected to meet special needs housing, and housing for low-income groups, however. The need for this type of housing will be indentified by local authorities. At the other end of the scale, housing associations must also provide more rented housing for higher income groups as well. They are to encourage more mixed income neighbourhoods. Less than 20% of housing in Rotterdam is owner-occupied, which is a lower percentage than in Amsterdam, and much lower than in the country as a whole. This does not necessarily mean that there are no middle-class people, but that there is a much stronger inclination to rent than to buy in the city. The city's aim is to provide more choice, for renting and buying.

New directions

By 1990 over 70 000 pre-war dwellings had either been renovated or demolished, about 60% of the total being renovations. The programme of renewal is by no means over. The city has earmarked another 50 000 for attention. The government, however, does not have urban renewal so clearly in its sights. The City has been offered a blanket sum to finish off the job, in place of a subsidy for each dwelling as in the past. The Council wants to complete the programme by 2005. Half of the provisional

15–20 000 new dwellings that the City Plan calls for should 'belong to the non-subsidized and partially-subsidized sectors'. More private housing in the urban renewal areas should be provided, but the main thrust must still be towards improving the housing of the poorer sections of the community.

Private-sector finance for housing has been creeping in over the last decade. Three luxury apartment blocks were financed by a big public-sector pension fund in the Waterstad. Social housing has also been built in the area but the point has been made that

> although new housing is dominated by the public sector, and although many public-sector apartments enjoy magnificent views of the port and river, it is noticeable that the few private-sector projects have almost all been allocated prime waterfront sites. Here, as in revitalization projects around the world, the alliance of capital and influence is evident, albeit on a restricted scale.[18]

Rotterdam, traditionally a working-class city with a policy bias towards care of the less advantaged, and a particular zeal for housing improvement, is having to juggle with choices which involves balancing the demands of those who want cheaper housing with the needs of the more mobile and more selective who the city is consciously seeking out to promote its economic aims. In the mixed commercial and housing development planned for the south bank, in the Kop van Zuid, private rented and housing for sale is fast being taken up in an area which was once scheduled totally for social housing.

Going for a mix

Rotterdam is relaxing its post-World War II policy of land use planning. Hitherto it has set aside specific zones generally for one category of property – offices or housing or industrial use, for example. Now the tendency is to follow the recent example of some North American cities like Baltimore and Boston and try to achieve a mixture of uses. Although some districts may be deemed primarily suitable for offices, planners want to leaven the use of land for a single activity.

Although the City Plan designates four areas as prime office locations, two are open to mixed developments. There was little which could be done about the other two because their construction is too far advanced. They are, first, Weena/Coolsingel (around Central station), where most of the 180 000 sq metres of prime office space in the city was under construction in 1992, dominated by the Nationale Nederlanden Bank building and, second, Churchillplein (at the other end of Coolsingel), anchored by the head offices of Robeco, the Dutch investment group. The greater flexibility will be evident at the other two locations, Blaak at the east end of Waterstad and Wilhelmina Pier in Kop van Zuid. Space on and around existing buildings along the boulevards in the area between the central station and Churchillplein will be used also for new office developments.

There is a further element in this attempt to enrich the city centre. Rotterdam has aggressively promoted cultural facilities to improve the quality of urban living. The focal point is the Museum Park, centred on the Museum Boymans-Van Beuningen, built before World War II the main art gallery. Two new museums have been built, one for architecture designed by Jo Coenen, which plans to serve architects around the world, and a second, the Kunsthal, for contemporary art exhibitions, designed by Rem Koolhaas, who runs the national Office for Metropolitan Architecture in Rotterdam. All of this highlights the changes and dilemmas for the city leaders.

> On the one hand, the Cultural Triangle aims to reinforce already existing qualities rather than aiming to create something new from scratch. On the other, it presents us with an example of the dilemmas that are inherent in urban regeneration strategies. One consequence of the implementation of the cultural strategy is to expel those forms of urban life that contradict the optimistic vision of 'the new Rotterdam'.[19]

Planning for the areas outside the central core of the city, classified as secondary activity areas, emphasize the economic role of Rotterdam as the pivot of the region, with the largest concentration of industry and its supporting services. These areas are drawn to reflect the highway, rail and metro junctions (existing and planned), on the north side, linking into the city on the one hand, and fanning out, on the other, to Amsterdam-south, Duivendrecht, Schiphol airport, Hoofdorp, Nieuw-Vennep, Leiderdorp, The Hague-East, Delft, and Rotterdam Region-North. On the south side, however, along the main highway and rail corridor, planners are seeking again to establish and control activities which strengthen the linkage between Rotterdam, its region and the hinterland. Along the Rhine-Schelde, which stretches north from Antwerp, by way of West Brabant and the Drecht cities to join the south side of the Rotterdam region, there is a strong environmental emphasis.

The key is that an expanded movement of goods is concentrated along main highways, the planned Betuwe rail freight link, and inland waterways. The movement of people will be by high-speed inter-city rail and internal rapid transit systems. Much of the rail infrastructure has still to be built. As the City Plan makes clear, 'environmental objectives cannot be reached without substantial expansion of public transportation', and that depends largely on national government funding. The private sector will also be expected to make some contribution.

Industrial sites are being made available on publicly owned land at the rate of about 60 hectares a year. In total, around 1000 hectares will be released over the next 15 years. Some 40% of this space has to be in and around the port. At the same time, the city is trying to regulate, in agrarian industrial zones, the largely unplanned spread, over large areas, of greenhouse cultivation. Such horticulture is an important employer of low-skilled workers but it is threatening to destroy the open country between Rotterdam, Gouda and The Hague.

Land lease

The City planners have an important tool in their bag with the huge land bank owned by the City, about two-thirds of the city area. The land bank was built up as the City bought sites for development which it then leased to the private sector or used for its own purposes. Land accumulation has not finished. The City even now is prepared to buy land, install infrastructure and then make it available to developers.

Leases reverted to the city on expiry, or, after negotiation with the leaseholder, when the site was required for a different purpose. The system did not encourage private developers; they felt that with leases sometimes as short as 25 years, it lacked stability. Since 1988, leaseholds have been granted for 99 years to make the system more attractive. The price at which the land is leased depends on its proposed use. Ground rents are indexed annually, with a review every ten years of the link between the rent and the value of the land, when a limit of 15% increase or decrease is set.

Anxious to reduce its own spending, the national government is encouraging municipalities to ration their release of land, in a bid to push up prices. Potentially higher profits from land sales could then be used to subsidize the cost of non-profit making ventures, like open spaces, museums and social housing.

The City's land holdings are managed by the Rotterdam City Development Corporation (except in the port, where land is managed by the Municipal Port of Rotterdam authority). The Corporation was set up in the late 1980s as a subsidiary of the Council, with equity of Fl 400m, and an instruction ultimately to become self-financing. It was given a wide brief to effect regeneration by promoting physical and economic renewal 'to make the city more international, competitive, diversified' (Gober Beijer, director, Dec. '92). Its brief enables it to cut through inter-departmental rivalries within the Council, and to work with major bodies that also have the economic development remit, like the port authority, and, indeed, with the private sector. One of its main concerns is that land is ready and available for business to move onto. It is a natural candidate for expansion on a regional basis under the wing of the new regional council.

The Port – fighting to stay on top

The port is still at the heart of Rotterdam's future, just as it was the life-blood of the city in the past. It is a living, breathing, day and night operation, highly mechanized, safe, efficient, but increasingly subject to competition from other west European ports. Rotterdam kicked off with the huge advantage of location, at the point where the Rhine-Maas empties into the North Sea. Linking the river with the North Sea is a deep man-made channel, the Nieuwe Waterweg. Started in 1864, its completion in the mid 1880s was a milestone in the development of the port. Postwar, the port expanded further downstream, shipyards were built, and the Europoort container terminal was constructed toward the mouth on reclaimed land. Likewise the Maasvlakte container terminal port which sits out in the North Sea. While ports around the world were dying in the 1960s and 1970s, because they could not meet the needs of the shippers – for reasons of investment capacity, labour inflexibility, and, of course, location – Rotterdam prospered.

Sometimes external circumstances determined Rotterdam's fortune. In the 1950s, the big oil companies were scurrying out of the Middle East and looking for strategic locations which promised stability. Rotterdam organized itself to meet the oil companies' needs. The oil companies expanded. Petrochemicals and other chemicals followed and have been a major component of Dutch exports. Another crisis – that of Suez and

Table 4.2 Total transshipments*: Rotterdam and world ports, 1989–92

	1989	1990	1991	1992
Rotterdam	292.5	287.8	292.0	293.1
Singapore	174.0	187.8	206.0	238.4
Kobe	167.2	171.4	174.1	169.7
Shanghai	146.0	139.5	146.7	163.0
Nagoya	124.8	128.9	136.8	131.8
Yokohama	119.0	123.8	121.9	122.4
Antwerpen	95.4	102.0	101.3	103.6
Hong Kong	85.4	89.0	104.5	101.0
Marseille	94.6	91.5	89.3	90.4
Kaohsiung	78.1	77.0	77.1	79.4
Hamburg	57.8	61.4	65.5	65.1

*million tons
Source: Port of Rotterdam

Figure 4.5 The port of Rotterdam: the base of past and future fortunes. *Courtesy of Freek van Arkel.*

the closure of the canal in 1956 – spurred the era of the supertanker. Rotterdam's deep water made the port eminently suitable to handle the giant vessels, and to build them, as at the Verolme yard, in the industrial Botlek port area.

Labour for the port and its dependent industry was recruited from all over the Rotterdam area, and from the islands to the south, as well as from outside the Netherlands. Labour was still in short supply, however. The oil and chemical multinationals were a powerful lobby which kept out anything else that would suck labour away from them. There had been a proposal to build a blast furnace to add value to the ore coming into the port, but this was abandoned in the face of their opposition.

Competitive forces

The port is no stranger to the threat posed by cheaper, efficient labour. The shipbuilding industry came under intense pressure from countries in the Far East, first Japan, then Korea. It succumbed finally in the late 1980s, and Rotterdam now only does ship repair and maintenance. Some of the facts about the port's competitive position were spelled out by an employer: organization of the labour force was too inflexible; labour disputes arising from wage demands were too frequent; costs had to be more competitive with Hamburg and Bremen, which were in a better position to take advantage of growth in eastern Europe; too much cargo with a relatively high added value which Rotterdam should be getting was going to Antwerp.[20]

Antwerp appeared to be competing strongly on charges, undermining to some extent the Rotterdam advantage of faster entry into the port. Rotterdam has the advantage that it can take very large ships, but this asset will lessen if smaller vessels take more business from very large crude oil and bulk carriers. In Rotterdam port circles, the belief is that German and Belgian port operators are being more heavily subsidized by their governments to invest in new technologies and logistics, as well as meeting a higher proportion of the costs of dredging that all of the North Sea ports depend upon.

Port Plan 2010

The port's response lies with the long-term plan painfully thrashed out between employers, unions, port management, and public authorities across the region. Port Plan 2010 is essentially about building an 'added value' port. The goal is to maintain and strengthen Rotterdam as a European 'mainport'. To realize this, commitments to continued investment in and outside the port need to be made by employers and the state. The plan is that the goods and materials which come into the port will be more valuable if they can have more done to them. Once a company commits itself to process material in the port, it is not going to jump off to another port which offers a bit off the charges.

Expansion of container traffic is the key. Rotterdam is one of the few ports in Europe which is sufficiently big and well equipped to take the

Table 4.3 Container transshipments*: major European ports, 1989–92

	1989	1990	1991	1992
Rotterdam	3.603	3.664	3.783	4.123
Hamburg	1.750	1.969	2.189	2.268
Antwerpen	1.510	1.549	1.761	1.835
Felixstowe	1.370	1.436	1.434	1.530
Bremen	1.249	1.198	1.264	1.308
Algeciras	412	397	762	780
Le Havre	900	860	918	746
La Spezia	454	413	464	612
Barcelona	448	440	489	552
Zeebrugge	288	334	303	525

* 1000 TEU's (Twenty Feet-Equivalent-Units)
Source: Port of Rotterdam

most modern container ships. Container traffic is diverse – most goods can now be transported in containers – which means that the customer base is more diverse. The port is therefore less dependent on the status of big industry sectors. Shipments of coal, for instance, were down by 17% in 1993 because of the downturn in German heavy industry.

But a lot more extra space for new terminals is needed – about 1000 hectares in the port's estimates. The major scheme is 'Delta Plan-8', where space is earmarked for eight new terminals on the edge of the port on reclaimed land. ECT/Sea-Land has already taken a similar terminal. The plots will be leased, on a phased basis, to other big shipping companies which will build their own terminals. When these are completed, capacity will be for around 2.5 million containers. The first plots were scheduled to have been prepared by 1995. Finance for the ambitious scheme comes from a mix of private and public-sector sources.

There is also a series of schemes for more general business activity. They involve the creation of centres where shippers and processors of particular products are being encouraged by the offer of space to form sector clusters. Fruit from Brazil, for example, is being turned into juice. The space is being created by filling in old harbours close to the city; relocating existing users like scrap metal merchants; and making more intensive use of existing sites. This should produce about 250 hectares of new space.

Pick-up points for the transporters are also being consolidated. At the moment, a barge collecting containers for shipment to customers might have to visit ten pick-up points. The plan is to centralize these collection points, so that they will have the same facilities being provided for rail users.

More advanced processing is being encouraged to locate in the port. Eastman Chemical Company in the United States, for instance, plans to invest Fl 1.2 billion in a specialist chemical plant to feed the European market. The investment will create 650 jobs.

Job losses in the port have been heavy. Between 1986 and 1990, some 10 000 jobs went due to the demise of shipbuilding, and the increase in container traffic at the expense of general cargo handling. The plan forecasts that employment will go up in the long term, but this will depend on the success rate in getting industry to expand. Port jobs as such are not scheduled to increase. The total cost of implementing Plan 2010, at current prices, exceeds Fl 100 billion.

The golden promise – the Kop van Zuid

Some 125 hectares on the south bank of the river Maas will become a new 'city' on the waterfront if the planners' most cherished plan comes off. The area was once a bustling part of the port but, by the 1980s, most of it was redundant. The planning team under their determined director, Riek Bakker, saw it as the one site which was large enough to realize their ambitions to provide Rotterdam with high-quality offices that could become the headquarters of overseas companies, and the homes and entertainment which would make Rotterdam the equal of many bigger cities.

The site had originally been intended to be used for social housing. The skill of Bakker – she is now planning adviser to the City Council – and others was to muster the support of the finance groups, and politicians. The city council then won the backing of government in the Hague for the scheme. Because Rotterdam was later on the scene, it had the benefit of hindsight, and was able to draw on the experiences of major waterfront developments in Baltimore and London.

There were three aspects to bringing the proposals to reality. First, there was the infrastructure, estimated to cost Fl 1500 million, both to open up the area and to link it with adjacent districts. So the Erasmus Bridge was commissioned, and new metro station and roads crossing the area will all be in place at more or less the same time as the first tenants move in.

Second, it was necessary to identify these tenants: they needed to have the substance which would offer the assurance of stability and economic growth in the area. They were largely found by the Dutch government, which will move in the city courts and tax offices and take up 70 000 sq. m. of the planned 121 000 sq. m. of office space in the first phase called Wilhelminapier. But, at the core of this phase is the Hotel New York, fashioned out of the old Holland-Amerika Line terminal. The first 500 homes were pitched at prices and rents aimed firmly at the middle-class market.

Third, the local community in adjacent districts had to be reconciled to the scale of the development and the arrival of new neighbours. The districts are some of the poorest in the city. The planners are determined to avoid the creation of the sort of social polarization which took place in London Docklands during the early and mid-1980s. Their approach is to train unemployed residents to work on the construction and to participate in the new local economy. The plans include some 2000 social housing units, a small number in the first phase but the majority on the eastern side of the site, closest to the existing districts.

The total development area will provide 400 000 sq. m. of office space, 5000 dwellings, a conference centre, a festival marketplace and river walkways. Already, however, the timetable has slipped; developers are reluctant to invest in the Kop Van Zuid when they have unlet office space in the central city.

The first architectural sketches of skyscrapers won the project the title 'Manhattan on the Maas'. The authorities, from the outset, wanted Kop Van Zuid to be an architectural showcase, mirroring the boldness of design which characterizes the Erasmus Bridge. An international consortium of architects, surveyors and contractors started in 1992 to work up the master plan for the Wilhelminapier.

A new 'city' in the north – Noordrand

The Integrated Plan for North Rotterdam (IPNR) reflects even more the long-term planning which Rotterdam can indulge in. This is a project for what is in effect a new city, dubbed in the promotion literature as 'the most important plan for spatial and economic renewal in the Randstad, besides that for Schiphol airport and the port plan'. The 30-year plan, called Noordrand, was construed around the city's belief that it needed a new airport which would replace the existing airport. This airport is unable to expand significantly because of noise pollution. To those who might think that Schiphol could serve Rotterdam's needs, the answer is that the new airport would have a different function, taking custom from the Hague, and the southern provinces of the country. It would be a regional airport, particularly suited for one-day business trips to other European cities, and in fact would complement the international hub of Schiphol.

Second, a phased commercial development would start with a new business complex of 200 000 sq. m., suitable for services, offices and light industry and taking in a research park, to be directed at international company type tenants. The environment would be suitable for port-related high-technology services which do not want to locate in the industrial surroundings of the port itself.

Third, a residential complex to the south of the proposed airport, would provide 7000 units – there would be the space for later expansion – of which 4000 would be single units for families, while 70% of the total would be unsubsidized housing.

Fourth, Noordrand would have a new highway, possibly tunnelled under the runway of the airport, to link with the existing trunk routes out of the port. The idea is to relieve congestion at one of the big bottlenecks on the A20, the main route to the hinterland of Europe.

Fifth, the planners want a proposed high-speed rail system between Brussels, Rotterdam Central Station, and (Schiphol) Amsterdam to have a station at Noordrand. In addition, there would be a new fast shuttle rail connection, using the same line, with Amsterdam, halving the current journey time, rail connections with Zoetermeer, on the outskirts of the Hague, and rapid transit connections with Rotterdam city.

In short, Noordrand would provide a major new business area north of Rotterdam which would relate to the rest of the Randstad. Its sponsors – Rotterdam council, government (Department of Transport) and Schiphol Airport (which would run the new airport) – see it as completing a new north–south axis with the Kop Van Zuid. By removing the present

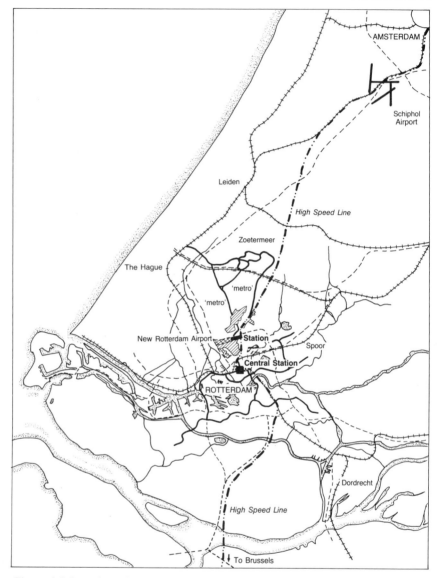

Figure 4.6 Location of proposed Noordrand. (▨ = Noordrand, – ·· – = proposed high speed line).

airport from its site, where noise levels prevent further residential developments, a huge new site in a high-quality area would be provided for the sort of middle-class housing which Rotterdam needs. The new airport was planned to accommodate a maximum of 2.7m passengers a year – 10% of Schiphol today – compared with the present airport which takes just 300 000 passengers annually.

The airport proposal provided an early stumbling block in the total plan. The Lubbers government, in power at the time of the plan's publication, had in principle accepted it, but then the section relating to the airport ran into the opposition of the environment minister. The new Rotterdam Council then split on the issue and ordered the plans to be re-evaluated. A decision is expected in Spring 1995.

4.3 SOCIAL INNOVATION (SOCIALE VERNIEUWING)

Social Innovation was dreamed up as the third arm of the City's plans, to complement physical and economic renewal. The concept was deliberately vague so that it would encompass many ideas, channelling them into specific programmes. It tilted the emphasis away from the provision for people by the state, to getting them to help themselves. This move towards self-reliance was in keeping with the moods of governments throughout the western world and, indeed, it was welcomed by the Dutch government. The skill of Social Innovation was that it managed to do this without politics and to do it humanely. It has been summed up in many phrases, but perhaps the most revealing in the original planning document was that policy emphasis had been too much on 'rights' and that there needed to be more talk about 'duties and responsibilities'.

The programme itself disappeared in spring 1994, deliberately, to avoid it spawning a bureaucracy. Its political proponents never wanted it any other way. Their goal was to plant the idea so firmly in the heads of the administrators and of ordinary people that it would happen without conscious consideration of the concept.

In 1986, the 'New Rotterdam' programme had been launched. This ushered in new office complexes, brought middle-class housing in the central city and put a new emphasis on cultural facilities. But there was a sizeable section of the population which could not relate to these and broader changes in society, since they were unemployed, sick, poor, old and immigrants who could not speak Dutch. Complaints, in one guise or another, came into the Town Hall daily. They amounted to accusations that the city was overlooking the needs of many of its residents, who noted that the streets were not any cleaner, that there were too many 'foreigners', and too much crime.

The search for answers had started among mayor and aldermen late in 1988. They called in advisers and academics for ideas. The city picked a bright, young bureaucrat, Gerard Kleijn, from the Office for Urban Renewal, to 'make a programme out of a concept'.[21] The director sought people from a variety of backgrounds to help him – people he judged to be 'innovative'. 'I started to accept ideas, not only to give them. I worked only temporarily with people – 2–3 months – we would disband, and they would go back to their organizations as ambassadors for the idea.' In 1990, the City got agreement with the government about the basic principles of what was shaping up as Social Innovation. Four policy areas were drawn up by the City – education, housing, employment and care. Residents as well as government, were to get on with making their lives better.

Kleijn did not believe the solutions lay in blaming government that it had caused the problems because it had cut funding to the city. Words like 'ghettos' and 'underclass' were banned. They might prise money out of the government but they made people frightened. It was important that the approach be linked to the way of thinking of the then new government: this tried to balance 'rights and obligations'. For example,

> the City Executive Committee believes that there must be an obligation to learn Dutch, as soon as the facilities exist for everyone concerned to follow a course; the long-term unemployed should have their unemployment benefit cut if they wrongfully refuse to carry out useful community work, and that Rotterdammers should be expected to make a contribution towards making and keeping the city clean and safe.[22]

Kleijn's team had to get the key sections of the community to participate. That included the police, employers, school heads, leaders of ethnic minority groups, politicians and bureaucrats. He did not expect all of them to come on board at the outset, however. 'Every innovation starts as a minority movement. If the minorities support each other and find a way to act, then it does not matter that the rest do not have a concept.'[23] Gradually, the police joined with the residents, even trusting people in the neighbourhoods to help fight crime and prostitution and make the streets more tranquil.

Neighbourhood action teams drew up their priorities ready to submit to the authorities for consideration. Initially, 100 streets were allocated Fl 3000 each, which could be spent as the teams decided – extra cleaning or policing, for instance. By the time the project wound up, and administration shifted from the city to the district councils, some 400 streets had become eligible. The streets were adopted as Opzoomer(Optimistic)straat, a word that crept into the language between people and bureaucrats.

Places were selected as 'coffee points' where aldermen came to meet the residents, turning round the usual process by which people with a concern went to see the aldermen. It was a salutary lesson for the local politicians: they found that frequently they were held in lower esteem than they had thought. Most of the residents' complaints were about safety, a common enough concern in most western urban areas. But in Rotterdam there was a particular edge: people in the inner city said that the suburbs should be made to take ethnic minorities. The residents were unhappy about the growing concentration of minorities in particular schools. Politicians found themselves trying to resist latent racism. Outside the conclaves of the coffee points, politicians argued that the inner city is, in fact, better adapted to immigrants, since it is more tolerant than the suburbs. The way to disperse ethnic minorities is to induce the suburbs to welcome immigrants rather than impose them.

The theme of Social Innovation is wrapped into specific programmes. One is the Project to Integrate Newcomers (PIN) which gives new arrivals to the city an introduction to the way in which Rotterdammers live. This is conducted in the language of the immigrant, who is then introduced to programmes of Dutch language and job training. Immigrants to the Netherlands are expected to adapt to being Dutch; the multicultural approach is not encouraged. But PIN can be used only by legal immigrants who register with the authorities. This excludes half of the newcomers to Rotterdam; the proportion which is believed to enter illegally.

Job Pools is one of several state schemes implemented locally to get the long term unemployed (three years out of work, or for ethnic minorities, two years) into the labour market. Jobs like caretakers are literally created. Recruits work for the job pool, which contracts with housing block management, for instance, to provide, say, janitorial services.

Another social programme, Social Return, means that people without skills should get a chance to benefit from the big projects planned for the city. It tries to co-ordinate training provision and job opportunities for long-term unemployed, particularly in projects initiated by the public sector. Over half of the unemployed in Rotterdam have been out of work for three years and more. The whole Kop van Zuid development area will provide a major test of the concept among the unemployed in the adjacent districts, where, in the early 1990s unemployment was running at around 40%.

The precedents are not wholly encouraging. Some of the problems encountered in training people to work in the construction sector were revealed in a pilot scheme which ran in Rotterdam during the late 1980s. First, the participants in the programme had to be trained actually to work. Most had not finished school, or they were among those immigrants who did not speak Dutch. Second, the programme was expensive, because highly experienced trainers had to be engaged and the period of training was lengthy. Third, employers were encouraged to take trainees by the offer of a subsidy, but Dutch employers, according to one of the organizers, tend to prefer to recruit trained people, or train them themselves, rather than be involved in government schemes. Fourth, on the side of the trainees, one of the main target groups, immigrants, are not enthusiastic about working in the construction sector. Notwithstanding these reservations, between 80 and 85% of the trainees were placed in jobs. The plan was to expand the scheme from construction to other sectors.

4.4 GOVERNMENT GOES UP AND DOWN

Major changes in the structure of government in the Rotterdam area will take place in 1997, the first significant changes in the pattern of administration since the early 1960s.

A new elected regional tier of government will cover Rotterdam and 18 surrounding municipalities. The functions of the new authority will be transferred up from the councils of the city and other municipalities. Within Rotterdam, services deemed best administered at local level are being transferred to 10 elected district councils, with population not greatly out of line with municipalities outside the city. These councils, initially set up as an experiment, now cover the whole city. The city council for Rotterdam will be abolished. The South Holland provincial authority for the Rotterdam-Rijnmond region will also disappear. The result will be to give the Rotterdam area two tiers of authority.

Change is not restricted to Rotterdam. Regional councils will be set up around the country, although they will not necessarily mirror the configuration of that for Rotterdam. The theory of Dutch local government is that the state adheres to the 'subsidiarity' rule, devolving responsibility to the lowest possible level, a principle that has subsequently been enshrined in the Maastricht Treaty establishing the European Union out of the European Community.

In practice, the working relationship between the state and local government in the Netherlands is so closely regulated as to stifle any initiative on the part of local government, according to critics. Most of the income of local authorities comes from the centre. The general fund for Rotterdam, for instance, is about Fl 1.1bn, of which the yield from property taxes is only Fl 250m. Separate pots of state money fund activities like education and urban renewal. Rotterdam has more leeway than most authorities, since it derives income from the port (Fl 20m) and Rotterdam City Development Corporation (Fl 15–20m).

> You have to give more freedom and money to the regional level . . . if you want to solve the problems, this has to be the decision . . . it is a big debate, because people in Parliament . . . for example, on secondary schools, talk about what teachers have to do between Monday morning and Friday afternoon! It is idiotic. Until recently, every week there were three papers from the ministry of education about what the teachers have to do, and what my colleague for education had to do . . . there is quite a lot of discussion about decentralization of power from central government, but it does not really exist at the moment.[24]

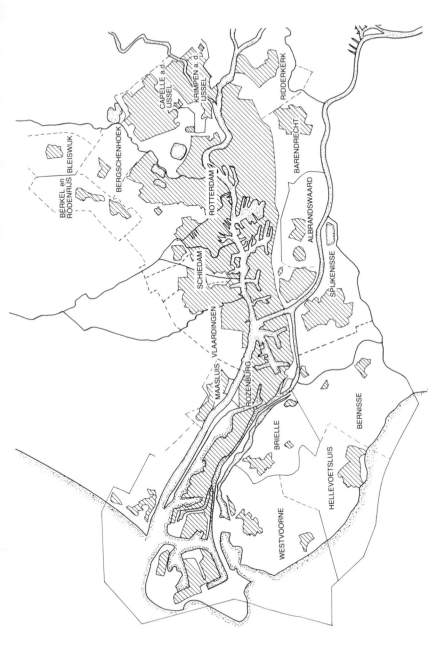

Figure 4.7 Area of new Rotterdam metropolitan government.

Rotterdam spearheaded earlier efforts at devising regional government, since a higher level decision-taking process had long been needed to resolve the physical, environmental and economic issues arising from the port. There was a proposal to annex all of the surrounding municipalities at one stage, but, apart from a minor expansion in the 1940s, this did not come about. In 1960, the huge growth in the port motivated creation of the Rotterdam-Rijnmond region, which comprised the city and surrounding urban area, and one rural area. The provincial authority had no brief to control port development, but it was required to devise policy for the effects of the port on the environment. So it had responsibility, but not power. It tended to speak for the weaker municipalities, since Rotterdam was powerful enough to lobby in the Hague on its own account.

It was again Rotterdam, not the Dutch government, which initiated steps to strengthen government in the region. The mayors of Rotterdam and its neighbouring municipalities set up a consultative council which published in 1991 a vague, but nevertheless controversial, plan for the future of the region. The Mayor of Rotterdam lobbied the Hague, which, with surprising rapidity, passed the necessary legislation for the new structure.

Central government had acknowledged that the existing government structure was lagging behind what was actually happening in Dutch cities.

> Economic activities do not take very much notice of municipal frontiers . . . In this country, an urban area consists of a large number of independent municipalities. Co-operation between these municipalities is usually based on a voluntary basis, limited to a few specific areas, and very time consuming, but with low productivity in terms of real decisions being taken . . . for major projects implementation of all the necessary procedures can take years. Stagnating decisions are in nobody's interest.[25]

The goal of government in sanctioning the new regional council is to reduce the time taken to reach decisions involving more than one authority. The goal of local government is to prise more power and finance from the state. Such aims are not mutually exclusive within the context of subsidiarity. Rotterdam is seeking from the central government the same degreee of latitude which, theoretically, it has been offering the district councils within its own sphere of authority. But decentralization in the city, however laudable in its notion of seeking to permit residents a closer identification with localized town halls, is also controversial. Some observers predict that issues like unemployment in the city will have to be addressed on a city-wide basis. With the demise of the City Council, it is not yet apparent how such issues will be handled.

4.5 AN UNEASY PARTNERSHIP

The partnership mechanisms which bring business and government together in the United States, and more recently in Britain, are much less developed in the Netherlands where governments only started to embrace the philosophy of market-oriented policies in the late 1980s. The long-established exception to the general rule is in Rotterdam, at the joint forum of port management and employers which meets regularly on issues of common interest. This forum is leveraged up into a lobby when required. There are, of course, other partnerships in the sense that major private sector investment is planned to complement public sector spending on upgrading the infrastructure and on the port itself.

The whole programme for the realization of Rotterdam's international aspirations depends on the market coming on board, following up lead developments like the museums and the creation of open spaces. The private sector must finance the construction of offices, business parks and housing. The success of the Kop van Zuid, and particularly Wilhelmi-napier, will depend crucially on the availability of private investment. Some will need to come from overseas pension funds, insurance companies and banks.

In the longer term, the private sector will be needed to make the Noor-drand plan work, possibly in helping with the planned extension of the metro. There are suggestions in the City Plan that private investors will be asked to contribute towards projects which traditionally the public sector has undertaken, including the provision of infrastructure and parks.

Social Rotterdam is also trying to secure a different sort of alliance with the business sector, to help solve long term social problems, and particularly to bring down unemployment levels. 'I do not think it [going to the private sector on social concerns] is in our culture. We started three, four years ago – not very long – to bring in this new approach. But we have to do it.'[26] So far, as would be expected, big employers have been more receptive than distinctly unenthusiastic small and medium-sized employers. Since they are the main source of new jobs, however, their co-operation has to be won. The council has approached shopkeepers' representative bodies, for instance, and asked them to consider that their members recruit from the pool of unemployed. Issues like the safety of the streets and crime have been raised. But, as a general comment, employers say 'is it really our problem? We pay our taxes.'[27]

The city council and the Chamber of Commerce took the unusual step of commissioning a study on the topic of partnership. ROTOR (Rotterdam Ontwikkelingsraad – Rotterdam Development Council) was a sort of think tank with representatives from business, education, science and technology and the administration. Its reports resulted in the formation of a working party on devising a strategy to bring more technology into different sectors of the city's economy, including the expansion of advanced technologies in the handling of goods at the port. This led to the port management being commissioned to draw up a strategy, to include public and private interest.

ROTOR was also asked to report on the possibility of establishing some common grounds for co-operation between government and business. The project, led by Professor Schuyt, reported in 1992. Its findings were damning of the government: clearly local politicians had made little effort to reach any accord with employers about what each side expected from the other. This, the report said, could be traced back to 'a lack of mutual trust'. It accused the politicians of not even understanding the way that the economy had shifted over the previous 15–20 years towards small and medium-sized companies.

In the past, the report said, 'something could be "arranged" quickly between a few large entrepreneurs and the council'. When it came to business sponsoring the arts or sport, that might still work. 'But in . . . the education/labour market, a policy for the ethnic minorities, the fight against unemployment and the living environment, other interaction processes are in order'.[28] The report called for:

- clarification of who is responsible for particular policies, including the split between the proposed government tier and the municipalities;
- companies to be given the feeling that they will get something in return for socially beneficial behaviour, if only by giving them the opportunities to stress their distinctive features and show their contributions to the public;
- an 'account manager' to be appointed on the public side with whom business can identify, for instance, on industrial estates;
- co-operative mechanisms to be constantly reviewed;
- government to help 'break a vicious circle' whereby companies had ceased to trust representative bodies, like trade groups, the Chamber of Commerce, organizations representing shopkeepers – 'introverted' business will not easily organize itself to liaise with government.

NOTES

1. *Institutions and Cities: The Dutch Experience* (1990) Netherlands Scientific Council for Government Policy.
2. Kreukels, A. M. J. and Salet, W. G. M. (eds) (1992) *Debating Institutions and Cities*, Netherlands Scientific Council for Government Policy.
3. Baartman, M. and Scheepens, J. (1993) *Economic Review*, ABN–AMRO Bank.
4. Pim Vermeulen, Alderman for Urban Planning and Housing, Rotterdam City Council, in interview with the author, January 1994.

5. Daniels, R. (1991) Rotterdam, city and harbour, *Cities* (*International Journal of Urban Policy and Planning*).

6. Bianchini, F. and Parkinson, M. (eds) (1993) *Cultural Policy and Urban Regeneration*, Manchester University Press.

7. *Institutions and Cities, op. cit.*

8. *Stadstimmeren, Rotterdam: 650 years* (1990) City Council.

9. Vader, J-W. Rotterdam City Development Corporation (1994) *Holland Herald*.

10. Browers, R. (1991) *Metropolis on the Maas*, Dutch Architectural Institute.

11. Ibid.

12. Morris, J. (1963) *Cities*, Faber & Faber.

13. Riek Bakker, director of planning, Rotterdam City Council, briefing to visiting delegation from Baltimore, December 1992.

14. White, P. (1984) *The West European City: A Social Geography*, Longman.

15. Len de Klerk, Policy Director, Rotterdam City Council, in interview with the author, January 1994.

16. Chris Jagtman, Director, Project Organisation in Urban Renewal, Stad, no date.

17. Ids Thepass, Manager, housing, Woningstichting 'Onze Woning', in interview with the author, December 1992.

18. Pinder, D. and Rosing, K. in B. Hoyle, D. Pinder and M. Husain (eds) (1988) *Revitalising the Waterfront: International Dimensions of Dockland Redevelopment*, Belhaven. .

19. Bianchini and Parkinson, *Cultural Policy and Urban Regeneration, op. cit.*

20. H. W. H. Welters, Director, SVZ (Board of port employers), *Rotterdam Daily*, 13 January 1994.

21. Gerard Kleijn, Project Director, Social Innovation. Interview with the author, December 1992.

22. City of Rotterdam (1991) *Social Innovation in Rotterdam*, December.

23. Kleijn, interview with author, *op. cit.*

24. Vermeulen, interview with author, *op. cit.*

25. van Rooy, Y., Minister for Foreign Trade and Regional Policy (1992) *Debating Institutions and Cities*, Netherlands Scientific Council for Government Policy.

26. Vermeulen, interview with author, *op. cit.*

27. Ibid.

28. Summary of report of ROTOR (since disbanded) translated into English for the author.

Toronto

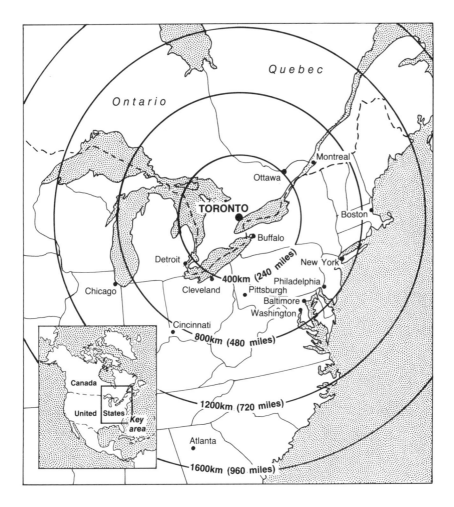

5

Figure 5.1 Toronto and the eastern Canadian and United States markets. *Source*: City of Toronto Planning and Development Department, 1992.

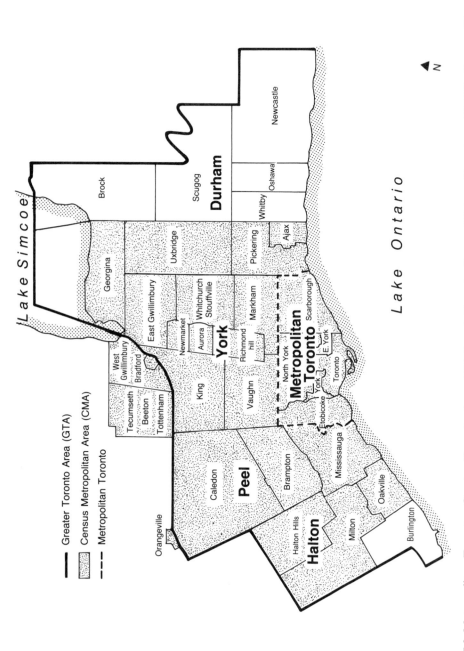

Figure 5.2 Metropolitan Toronto, Greater Toronto Area (GTA) and Toronto Census Metropolitan Area (CMA). *Source:* City of Toronto Planning and Development Department, 1992.

Table 5.1 Basic facts about Toronto

(a) Population (1991)

Metropolitan Toronto[1]	Toronto CMA[2]	Greater Toronto Area[3]
2 275 771	3 893 046	4 230 000

Notes:
1. 6 municipalities.
2. 'Economic region', comparable to Primary Metropolitan Statistical Area in the US.
3. Metro Toronto and the Regional Municipalities of Durham, Halton, Peel and York.

(b) Ethnic minorities in Metro Toronto

Year	Percentage of population
1986	20.7
2001 (forecast)	28.4

(c) Percentage labour force with university education: 27% (GTA)

(d) Employment by sector, Toronto CMA:

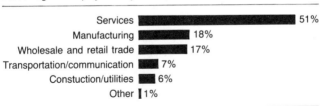

Percentage of employment by sector, 1992

- Services 51%
- Manufacturing 18%
- Wholesale and retail trade 17%
- Transportation/communication 7%
- Constuction/utilities 6%
- Other 1%

(e) Top five companies (by employment)
1. General Motors of Canada Ltd
2. Canadian Imperial Bank of Commerce
3. Bank of Nova Scotia
4. Bell Canada
5. Hudson's Bay Company

5.1 INTRODUCTION

A temperate melting pot

Arriving in Toronto from American cities is a pleasure. Immediately, the city feels more relaxed. The absence of tension between races is in stark contrast to the black and white split in some towns in the United States, and sometimes between minorities, or the fear that is increasingly surfacing between new and native-born Europeans. Neither does Toronto flaunt obvious extremes of wealth and poverty. Public services – schools, transport – are used to some degree by everybody. The schools are not plagued by drugs and violence. These observations, however, have to be qualified. At first glance it is a demi-paradise. But there are inequalities in wealth and opportunities which give rise to a miniature version of the difficulties and needs in cities over the border.

The Toronto area has expanded rapidly in population and jobs in the last 30 years, spilling out far beyond the boundaries drawn around the metropolitan area in 1953. Then, it was the commercial capital of Ontario. Now it is the premier city of eastern Canada which accounts for one-quarter of the nation's gross domestic product. It is also a much more enjoyable city. Where it was described as the dullest city in Christendom, tourism is today a fast growing industry.

It used to be smart for all and sundry to dub Toronto as dull. Sunday in the city was symbolic of its strong Protestant ethic of all work and no play. 'All stores and movies, everything with a door on it, closed up tight', recalls David Lewis Stein, *Toronto Star* columnist. In 1950, an alderman, Alan Lamport, promoted the plebiscite to allow sports on Sunday. 'Clergymen, newspaper editorial writers and, it seemed, everyone important in the city was vilifying Lamport.'[1]

But the important people did not get their way. Toronto got its sport on Sunday (although it was another 40 years before it was permitted Sunday trading). It could not change its climate – damp cold in winter, humid in summer – but just about everything else has changed. Now Toronto boasts theatres, international film festival and a baseball team – the Blue Jays – which won the world series in 1992. The team's home base at the SkyDome at the foot of the famous CN Tower downtown, seats 50 000 baseball fans. Finished in 1989, complete with retractable roof and surrounded by a hotel, restaurants and other entertainments, it quickly gave the city a much needed new marketing symbol in the international arena.

But it also symbolized the 1980s 'dash to spend' when Toronto was enjoying an unprecedented economic boom, which was followed by the 1990s' dive into recession. Love or hate its brooding appearance, the taxpayers of Ontario are stuck with a debt that, at the last count, had risen to over C\$350m. The stadium was making an operating profit but 'couldn't even begin to pay back the construction loans ... Debt no longer seemed like such a magical way to create wealth.'[2]

It was in the 1960s that the New City Hall, its two curved towers still strikingly original a quarter of a century later, and its paved plaza ice rink, marked the turning point in the image of the city. This had been a city in which people could prosper, but nobody much took it seriously as a city. But here was a futuristic building, in contrast to the traditional style of what became old City Hall, which signalled to the rest of the world that Toronto wanted notice taken of it.

More remarkable was the broadening ethnic mix of the population. Once predominantly, even aggressively Protestant, and British – the 'Orange Lodge' from Protestant Ulster was reputed to have run the town – post war Toronto became the destination for a new wave of immigrants, Catholic, and Jewish, from Portugal, Italy and eastern Europe. In 1961, 96% of the population of Toronto CMA (Census Metropolitan Area) still had European roots. But the proportion of the population with non-British origins had grown to 39%, from 31% in 1951.

Then the newcomers were arriving from the developing world, particularly from South Asia, Africa, South America, the Caribbean, more recently from eastern Europe, the former Yugoslavia, and Hong Kong. By 1986, the Census revealed 20.7% of the population of Metro Toronto as having racial minority origin. Moreover, this is an under-count, since people born in North America and Europe of racial minority parentage

Figure 5.3 Fruit, vegetables and smiles in Toronto, a latterday haven for migrant Asian labour and capital. *Courtesy of Metropolitan Toronto Convention and Visitors Association.*

are not included. A report by Metro Toronto in 1990[3] estimated the proportion would rise to 28.4% in 2001.

The immigrants were mostly anxious to be Canadian, and were understandably indifferent to Toronto's British connection. Ontario province tended to take about half of the immigrants into Canada, and Toronto about half of the Ontario number, although this has sometimes been higher. Immigrants have been the major source of population growth in Canada. The latest wave is the Hong Kong Chinese. Over 300 000 have come to the city so far. Many are able to buy property, and invest in business, on entering the country. Some have settled permanently, but as Canadian law allows them to retain dual nationality, others are using their investment in Canada as a foothold if they should decide to return.

The transition from the dominant white, Protestant culture to a lively mix of cultures and colour within the space of a generation had been achieved relatively painlessly, at least until the recession of the early 1990s, making Toronto the envy of other cities. It has also largely avoided dereliction of older parts of the city. So Toronto streets, car parks, schools, public transport, are relatively safe, which constitutes no mean marketing point played to encourage tourists and inward investment.

Toronto's business sector, meanwhile, is turning its attentions to the United States rather than Europe. Commerce and industry in the city has been through a period of transition over the last decade reflecting the adaptation forced on managers and workers to increase productivity and competitiveness, and cut Canada's high production costs. Toronto has consolidated its position as the most important centre for financial services in Canada. The Stock Exchange has expanded the volume of trading and diversified into new investment forms.

The strengthening connections with American business now goes far beyond the branch plant syndrome that left Canadians feeling dominated by their big brother. Now, the American contacts are actively solicited in one direction, while Canadian companies are becoming takeover targets. The Reichmann Brothers – two ambitious and highly successful Toronto property developers until the downfall of their company, Olympia & York, in London Docklands – launched their Battery Park project in New York on the back of their successful Toronto venture. Property, along with Ontario's more traditional interests in minerals, were fuelling speculative interest with recovery in the Canadian economy.

Toronto today, like most cities, has been shaped by a variety of influences and factors, fortuitous and planned. In the planned category was the tier of government set up in 1953 to integrate the suburbs and the city. Toronto was the model for American advocates of metropolitan government as a solution to the urban ills that can be attributed in part to the tight boundaries of their city.

New answers are needed

The two-tier system of government in Toronto, however, has not kept pace with the main thrust of population growth beyond its administrative limits. The areas grouped into four regions surrounding metropolitan (Metro) Toronto sprawl just like the worst American suburban offenders. The population in these regions was 1.86m in 1991, against 2.15m in Metro, but growing rapidly while the population of Metro is static.

The big difference from the United States is that so far, Toronto itself has not capitulated to the catastrophe of inner-city blight. Although business and families have moved out of Metro Toronto, attracted by the space and property taxes which are at least one-third lower, many middle and high earners prefer to stay in the city. The less well-off are concentrated in what were the new suburbs 40 years ago. Metro Toronto's capacity to avoid the impoverishment that beset inner urban areas in the United States in the 1960s and 1970s is hindered by budget problems at the all-important level of the province. Toronto was well served by provincial and Federal financial support until recently. The failing of the provincial government, however, was identified as far back as 1964 by Hans Blumenfeld, architect of a plan for the cohesive growth of Toronto: 'unusually strong provincial intervention' would be needed, he wrote[4] to implement the plan. It did not materialize, as will be elaborated later.

5.2 THE NEW SUBURBS

It was to the credit of the original proponents of government of city and suburbs in the early 1950s that their creation stood the test of time as far as they went. The expectation, however, that the boundaries would be expanded with the physical expansion of the city was not fulfilled. Instead, the province created government for four regions which with Metro comprises the GTA (Greater Toronto Area), an administrative unit which has no authority vested in it. The area of the GTA represents almost half of the province's wealth and population. If it had been consolidated into a single unit of government it could have comprised a powerful presence in the government of the province.

Metro Toronto has no control over the growth of the new suburbs, a fact which could increasingly weaken its authority.

In spite of Metro Toronto's success . . . the limited spatial extent of its authority remained a source of weakness in the early 1980s and promised to undermine further the effectiveness of metropolitan government. While Metro's boundary remains unchanged and the metropolis continues to spill across the boundary there are serious questions regarding the spatial effectiveness of the system.[5]

The population in these outer suburbs grew by 4% annually between 1971 and 1991. Much of the land was farmland. Only 16% is currently urbanized, against 98% in Metro. Densities are much lower even in the areas that are classified as urban, at less than half that in the metropolitan area. But, on the basis of current trends and given the availability of space, well over half (3.8m) of the population of GTA (6m) in 2021 will live in the new suburbs.

Suburbs are not a phenomenon of the twentieth century. As far back as the Middle Ages, the suburb was a reality. They represented the extension of the town beyond its walls. There have been some highly reputable critics of the suburbs. The venerated planner, Lewis Mumford, and others, cast suburbs as the villains which sucked wealth out of the city. On first seeing Toronto (where she now lives) the celebrated urban writer, Jane Jacobs, found even the earlier suburbs 'quite as baffling physically and incoherent socially as their counterparts anywhere, and fully as ecologically destructive and as ill-suited to service by public transportation'.[6]

The Canadian Urban Institute catalogues the environmental costs of the later suburbs which have

> produced dependence on the automobile, consequent traffic congestion and high energy consumption, increasingly insupportable demands for expensive road, sewer, and water systems, dramatic losses in the amount of land under cultivation, and social and economic segregation by limiting housing to single-family homes.[7]

Markham – a suburb facing critical choices

Planners in some of the outlying suburbs see things differently. Theirs is a campaign to bring some order and form into the sprawl. They see the suburbs as the competitive 'cities' of the future. The residential and business occupants pay low taxes compared with Metro taxes, despite their relative affluence. But the cost of providing infrastructure and basic services to the scattered homes and commercial centres is growing. And even suburban residents get older, and need social services. Markham is one of the authorities that decided to plan now.

Population 161 000, it begins where Metro Toronto and the subway line ends, due north of the city. Houses in spacious lots dot both sides of the highway. Areas of scrubland are punctuated by clusters of offices, that accommodate the finance houses, and international communications and computers companies, which have become household names – IBM, Apple – as familiar as the washing powders, drink and food producers became in the 1950s and 1960s. The town is home to 90 000 jobs. With its office parks, retail parks, shopping malls, all built for the car user, Markham is, unashamedly, what geographers term an 'edge city', its expansion spurred by its proximity to two main highways. Markham sits astride highway 404, running north from Toronto to the Lake Simcoe area and north Ontario hinterland, and highway 7 which cuts across east to west. A little to the south will be a new cross highway, 407, the first toll highway in the province, to relieve congestion on 404.

Population and jobs in the town have soared in the last 20 years. The Toronto-Centred Region Plan forecast in 1970 that the town would have a population of 20 000 by 1990. It had five times that number by 1985. By 2011, the population is forecast at 325 000, equivalent to one of the six authorities which make up the metropolitan Toronto area.

Plans for Markham's future

Markham got going on a series of studies, plans and conservation exercises to bring shape and form to the town. It had already pitched for the Olympics Village in Toronto's bid for the 1996 Olympics. The town credits a former mayor – the late Anthony Roman who hailed from a successful east European business family in the area – with the inspiration to initiate the planning exercise. Lorne McCool was hired to manage the process, which he sees as 'a magnificent opportunity to significantly change the existing pattern of development in a meaningful way'.[8] A planner formerly working within the Metro area, he is now dismissive of what he terms the Metro 'consensus' approach to government as 'slow, and inappropriate to the suburbs'.

Andres Duany and Elizabeth Plater-Zyberk, their reputation in projects like Seaside Village in Florida, were commissioned to lead a team to produce the master plan which was unveiled in mid 1994.

The new centre will be located between highway 7 and the proposed highway 407, and McCowan Road to the east. The main geographical focus is the Rouge River which runs through the site, and is planned as a preserved area of countryside. An earlier study of natural features in Markham had warned that much of the natural landscape was in danger of being lost. The total area is around 800 hectares, which, crucially, is in a planning area that came under the jurisdiction of the province in 1978. New villages, complete with village halls, shops, schools, parks, are planned to the east and west of a 'multi-activity' core, that includes residential. Total commercial space is over 7m sq. ft, retail 1m sq. ft, 15 150 dwellings for 36 000 people. The main focus of the core is a wide boulevard. The whole design concept of the master plan is 'neo-traditional', even classical for public buildings.

One village would provide a mix of 'merchant's houses' (retail, services

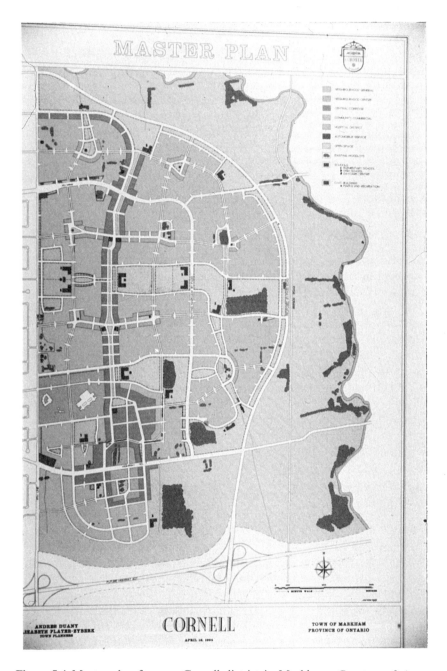

Figure 5.4 Master plan for new Cornell district in Markham. *Courtesy of Anares Duany, Duany Plater-Zyberk Assocs.*

Figure 5.5 Markham: a Toronto outer suburb plans a centre to match its growing ambitions. *Courtesy of Andres Duany, David Jansen, WORR Partnership, Michael Morrissey.*

businesses and residential), workshops, apartment buildings resembling manor houses, row houses, link houses, suburban houses, and big houses. By mixing residential, commercial and retail, the need for most journeys to be made by car – as is now the case – will be reduced. Another – Cornell – is planned to the east of the centre, with traditional type housing, most dwellings being within a five-minute walk of a neighbourhood or village centre. Again, the reduction in car journeys is a prime target.

The total impact of the plans on housing densities would be to reduce low-density from 80% of the total down to 60%, creating 15% high-density, and 25% medium density. Some new housing will be in the 'affordable' category. Provincial guidelines call for 30% of new projects to include cheaper housing and subsidized co-operatives.

Not in my backyard

People living in Markham and other outlying suburbs, however, tend to like things as they are. They did not move to Markham to save money – even a so-called 'affordable' dwelling is around $160 000 – but for space and safety. They see both disappearing if they capitulate to the ideas of the planners, and taxes being pushed up to pay for services for the poorer people who would occupy these dwellings. It is exactly the same argument that was rehearsed, and lost, in the 1960s and 1970s, across most of North America.

So Markham planners organized three big public meetings on the original concept plans, followed up by technical workshops, to build up a consensus. The business community is more supportive, because it wants better public transport, and housing at prices which will swell the small pool of unskilled and semi-skilled workers.

Raising taxes

Towns like Markham will have to put up property taxes. The need for community services is on the increase, for the young and old. The over 65s are the fastest growing age group, yet out-of-town type developments like Markham are designed mostly with the young and middle-aged in mind. More investment is needed to provide the 'hard' services – piped water, sewage collection and local roads. (The regional authorities – York, in this case – look after water purification and sewage treatment.) Councils in the past might avoid levying the full cost of providing these services, and get bailed out finally by the province. Rescue of that sort is no longer a possibility.

The tax question within the Toronto region has become an acrimonious issue. Commercial and industrial taxes are on average 37–44% lower in the four regions outside Metro, causing some councils in the Metro to initiate legal action on their neighbours. The Metro authority is linking the issue to the wider question of the competition between Toronto and other centres in Ontario, and American city regions.

The outlying suburbs, again, see things differently. They are not only competing for business to relocate from Metro but also looking all the time at the tax levels set by other outer councils. Markham sees itself vying with Mississauga, for instance, which has the added benefit of the city's main airport within its boundaries. More development and therefore a wider tax base has been the traditional way of keeping taxes down. But Markham went into the 1990s with at least a quarter of its new

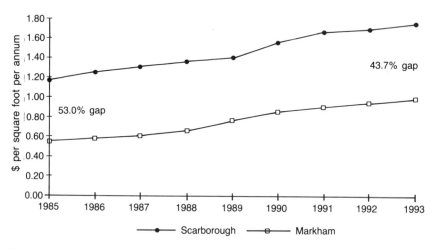

Figure 5.6 Industrial realty tax gap Scarborough (Metropolitan Toronto) and Markham. *Source*: The Toronto Real Estate Board; Insight Magazines.

commercial stock unlet and unsold – less than many places, but high enough to halt any more new developments for a while.

In the longer term, a well-planned, mixed-use town is believed be to the answer. But it is long-term. The master plan for the town centre could take between 30 and 50 years to realize, say officials. Within that period, the town would hope that its intentions would win over the province to rethink the viability of financing an extension to the Toronto subway out to Markham.

5.3 METROPOLITAN GOVERNMENT

Mixing growth and social equity

Toronto's tier of government for the metropolitan area which dates from 1953 can be seen as an attempt almost unparalelled in North America to manage growth and achieve some degree of social equity across a wide area. The city after World War II had embarked on a period of economic growth which continued for a generation. The city expanded physically to accommodate growing population and commere. But, having set up metropolitan government, the province later shrank back from stretching the boundaries to include the area that was developing on the fringes. The province had various stabs at the issue, but always recoiled from giving the commissions of inquiry the terms of reference which would allow it to be properly investigated.

In the early 1970s, the province was more occupied with the idea of regional than metropolitan government. Four regions were thus created on the outskirts of Metro Toronto – Durham, Halton, Peel and York. They were 'more timid creatures than had been envisaged'[9] by the commission, and the committee of parliamentary members which had endorsed regional government for the province. Most of the other proposed regions were never set up. In the 1980s, the province looked again at the options for Metro Toronto: to extend the boundaries, and turn it into a regional government; to form a new authority and dissolve Metro; to set up a framework for the area which did not bind any of the authorities. The last was settled upon, and a co-ordinating committee of 35 municipalities set up, but only with advisory powers.

And so the Office of the Greater Toronto Area was born in 1988. Gardiner Church, then a senior official in the provincial government, was appointed to run the GTA. 'We had no mandate, no tools. We quickly realized that our only tool was to raise awareness. So three years was spent warning cataclysmically about what would happen if we did not address the problems.'[10]

From that campaign came a study by consultants which set out three possible futures for the region.[11]

The three options

'Spread' – continue along the trend, described in the report as 'closest to the status quo in terms of delivery of new housing, lifestyles, and government planning/regulation affecting urban development', but also described as the least compatible with sustainable development. It was, however, the least risky since it required no change.

'Central' – concentration of growth in existing communities in central, built-up areas, which would be the most efficient solution in the use of land, and energy, but would require the greatest amount of government regulation to direct population growth from suburban areas to the centre.

'Nodal' – also to build on existing communities, and their urban infrastructure such as civic buildings, commuter rail stations, etc. while providing for continuing growth in the suburbs at higher densities.

The study made no recommendation, but the nodal concept was clearly the most acceptable, and was accepted as planning guidance by the majority of municipalities in and outside metropolitan Toronto.

Metro's evolution

The legitimacy of municipal government in Canada goes back to the late eighteenth century when the country was being settled from Europe, but it was the Baldwin Act, passed in 1849, which established that municipalities should be the major provider of government services. This ended up with the city of Toronto, at least until the early part of this century, having a larger budget than the whole of the government of Ontario. The 1930s saw a switch towards more power being concentrated at the provincial and Federal levels, however, as the Depression found the municipalities unable to meet their obligations to foot the bill for the burgeoning welfare payments.

The city of Toronto, meanwhile, had been expanding its jurisdiction. In the 1880s to World War I, annexation of neighbouring communities was the means. Later, it adopted incorporation of neighbouring municipalities. By the 1930s, the city had a population of over 620 000, the 12 surrounding suburbs totalled 162 000. The first calls for a metropolitan-style government were already being made, in response to growing inequities in the provision of services, notably education, and mounting financial difficulties that were being experienced in some municipalities. The moves were halted by World War II. By 1949, the city had 673 000 people, a bit less than immediately postwar, while the suburbs – 'some of them densely populated and cities in everything but name'[12] – had shot up to 348 000. Two years later the suburban tally was 442 000. In one year alone – 1951 – the population of one suburb (North York) had gone up by 30% to 85 897. The pattern of the suburbs outstripping the city was well under way.

But in everything from water supply to education, services in the suburbs were inferior to those in the city. Between 1949 and 1951, a series of reports by the Civic Advisory Council of Toronto – the product of 'a major "joint effort" on the part of the metropolitan political community'[13] since they were sponsored by some suburban as well as city leaders – documented the problems and advocated metropolitan government as the solution.

The Cumming Report helps establish metropolitan government

The Cumming Report which initiated metropolitan government was published two years later, following the judicial hearing chaired by Lorne Cumming QC before the Ontario Municipal Board of two applications:

1. The city of Toronto had applied to the Board to amalgamate the 12 municipalities and create a single, centralized government, which would involve 'the complete dissolution of the existing local governments'.[14]
2. The town of Mimico, one of the municipalities, wanted a joint administration to be set up which would provide several key services like education, planning and sewerage. Cumming described this as an alternative which would have the effect of 'a sweeping reduction of the powers and responsibilities of the various local authorities and the creation of a new type of central authority'.[15]

It was for the applicants to satisfy the Board of the inadequacies of the existing system, then to convince the Board that changes 'can be reasonably expected to provide an adequate solution'.[16] Neither applicant succeeded in convincing the Board of their chosen courses. It was significant, however, that 'they have clearly established the urgent need for some major reform of the existing system and the Board has so found.'[17]

Cumming strikes a balance

The Cumming Report, a model of clarity and simplicity in official reports, recommended that a tier of metropolitan government which would have exclusive responsibility for services such as water supply and distribution (with the power to delegate to an appointed Metro utilities commission), sewerage and drainage, metropolitan highways, parks, education (co-ordination) and public transport. Other services would be handled at the level of the lower tier municipalities. Metro would also be given assessment and taxation powers, the property taxes collected by the municipalities to be paid to Metro for the services provided by it, and exclusive power to borrow and issue debentures on its own credit. The

Table 5.2 Responsibilities of Metropolitan Toronto and City of Toronto Councils

Metropolitan Toronto Council	City of Toronto Council
Community services	
Police	Fire protection
Ambulance	
Emergency services	Public health
Public transportation	Electricity distribution
	District heating
Water purification	Water distribution
Sewage treatment	Sewage collection
Waste disposal	Water collection
Major roads	Local roads
Regional parks	Local parks
	Community centres
Cultural activities	Cultural activities
Public housing	Public housing
Licensing of business	Inspection of buildings
	Historical preservation
Regional planning	Local planning
Reference library	Public libraries
Exhibition centre	
Zoo	

Source: Canadian Urban Institute.

last provision meant that a system was being set up which would allow the suburbs to finance their necessary infrastructure on the credit rating of the city.

Compared with city government in the United States, although not compared to another upper tier council, for instance, the old London County Council, the powers assigned seemed substantial. Not so, according to one commentator:

the division reflected a somewhat limited view of metropolitan government. Only one function, public transport, was wholly allocated to the metropolitan level whereas several, such as police and fire protection, remained wholly within local jurisdiction.[18]

Responsibility for the police, which was a significant step, was given to Metro later. The Metro Council would not be elected by the people but made up of representatives nominated from the constituent municipalities.

The Cumming Report was both cautious and forward-looking on the issue of boundaries. It recognized that there would almost certainly need to be an extension at some stage, but ruled out any suggestion that it try to determine new boundary limits for some future stage of development. The caveat was: 'provided that the boundary recommended in the initial period is deemed a temporary boundary only and that there is no repetition of the errors of the past in neglecting to provide for future growth'.[19]

Accordingly, the new Metro Council was to be given a degree of land use planning control over areas described as 'fringe', the actual areas to be determined in consultation with the provincial planning ministry. The outcome was that the Metropolitan Toronto Planning Board was set up with advisory planning powers over a substantial territorial area – a sort of regional planning body, but without teeth.

Metro becomes a reality

Metro Toronto was set up by an act of the provincial government in 1953, following immediately on the publication of the report. It was a deftly executed political move by Premier Leslie Frost, a small-town lawyer who was not at all enamoured with Toronto. He faced opposition. Some critics said that Toronto was being set up to take over the world. But Metro came about because of the dominance of the ruling party in the province. Their political persuasion was conservative, they were mainly Protestant, and British, but they instituted a framework of government designed to promote equity in public services, in a city which came to accommodate a diversity of cultures and race.

Metro's heyday

The first chairman of Metro appointed by the provincial government was Frederick Gardiner, already respected in local affairs, whose reputation grew considerably over the next seven years as he managed to exploit the divisions and parochialism of the municipalities to enable Metro to carry out its programme.

The first review of Metro[20] had been planned when Metro was set up in 1953. Cumming carried out the review. He gave Metro the green light and recommended that responsibility for the police be given to Metro, which was adopted. In retrospect, these now look like the golden days for Metro. The suburbs were endowed with 'the longest sewer pipes in the world were laid, roads were paved from dirt tracks, all opened up for development, resulting in the lowest cost housing in North America'.[21] There have been more restrained judgements, but

> there were considerable achievments in these early years. The backlog in water supply and sewer services that had become so critical was dealt with quickly and effectively; these services were further extended

in order to facilitate the construction of housing for a growing population.[22]

But 'by the early 1960s the operation began to run out of steam and pressure for further reforms mounted'.[23] In 1963 the city of Toronto applied again for amalgamation of the 13 municipalities. (The city, which nominated half of the representatives to Metro, was in an increasingly anomalous position since it accounted for less than 40% of the population.) The provincial government appointed a one-man commission to look at Metro in 1965 which sought to address the issue of population growth and representation in the suburbs by proposing that the 13 municipalities (including the city) be consolidated into four units of government, which would be large enough to 'perform a significant government role'.[24] All four units would be given the designation of cities. By enlarging the city of Toronto, the 50/50 representation balance could be maintained.

Coping with growth and changing responsibilities

On the issue that was to dog the later years, that mid-1960s report had acknowledged that the fringe areas were growing already faster than Metro, but no recommendation was made to extend the boundaries of Metro on the basis that the municipalities in these areas were still too small to be put on anything like the same sort of footing as the municipalities within Metro. The reorganization was implemented in 1967, varying slightly from the recommendations: six cities were formed – Etobicoke, North York, Scarborough, East York, York and Toronto, the same as they are today. The city of Toronto's representation on Metro was reduced to 40%. The new framework significantly altered the appearance of metropolitan government but 'it did not lead to a rejuvenation of Metro and its programmes'.[25]

Metro was also given responsibility for community services, turning it increasingly towards being a provider of services for people rather than concentrating on infrastructure. Also in 1967 a committee set up by the province – the Smith Committee – recommended a reorganization of municipal government in Ontario. (It had started out by reviewing provincial and municipal taxes, but had come to the conclusion that financial reform could not be effectively undertaken without a complete restructuring of the municipal system in the province.[26]) This was the report that led to the four outer regions being constituted between 1971 and 1974.

These new municipalities tended to become strengthened county governments without new powers from the province and, particularly in what became known as the Greater Toronto Area, without geographic boundaries that corresponded to the growing urban region.[27]

Yet another review into Metro, conducted by a former provincial premier, John Robarts, reported in 1977. He assessed Metro partly on the basis of its economy and effectiveness – criteria which were used increasingly to measure local government performance in the 1980s. He found the system wanting in certain respects, but he did not propose radical changes to the structure. He did recommend that members of Metro be elected, however – this came into effect finally in 1988, the same year that the Office of the GTA was set up.

The fact that these later reviews were ordered was a mark of the concern that the concept of metropolitan government should be amenable to being expanded in line with the physical growth of the area which remains oriented on the city, or else abandoned in place of something new. But there was a reluctance on the part of the provincial politicians to see through what they were almost certainly thinking. The seat of the provincial government is actually in Toronto, but that did not seem to make it any easier for the politicians to understand the city.

Planning issues in the region

Toronto was the topic for an ambitious economic and land use plan produced by a team of planners led by Nigel Richardson, working with Hans Blumenfeld, a radical thinker who could envisage that Toronto would need to move towards planning on a regional scale, and Darcy McKeough, appointed minister of municipal affairs for the province in 1967. They produced the Toronto-Centred Region Plan (TCR) released in 1970.

It was intended as one of several covering parts of Ontario, which 'set the framework for urban development, green space protection, and infrastructure investment for the remainder of the century'.[28] The Toronto Plan aimed to control the desire of developers to spread north of Toronto, along the Yonge Street corridor, and west. This was to be effected by concentrating development more on an east–west line configuration anchored between Oshawa and Hamilton, with Toronto as the first-order or primate centre, and nominating a broad tract in the north to remain predominantly rural. The plan, in the end was not decisive. 'It was never abandoned, but it languished.'[29]

Developers who had already put together parcels of land in the northern corridor in anticipation of getting planning permissions found that their lobbying of politicians succeeded. 'Any restraint to development north of Metro in the Yonge Street corridor was lifted.'[30] The Metropolitan Toronto Planning Board, set up at the start of Metro government, had already had its sphere of influence reduced, and in 1975, the Board was wound up. The results of the failure of politicians to adhere to outline land-use planning concepts can be seen in the ragged development marching across this corner of Ontario.

Metro Toronto has started to take planning guidance more seriously in its territory, resulting in the publication of the Metro Strategic Plan draft. Any momentum for the province to come up with a new initiative diminished with the election of the New Democratic Party (NDP) to the province in 1990. The 'left-wing' (in Canadian parlance) party's success was precipitated by the desire for change among the electorate, but it had not been expected, least of all by the party's leaders. Much of its time has been spent reconciling the agenda of its supporters in the unions, and lobbyists for improvements in social services, with the demands of business that government help rather than hinder progress, as did Premier Bob Rae's strong opposition to the 1989 free trade agreement between the United States and Canada.

The biggest constraints on the government, however, have been imposed by the legacy of its predecessors in the form of a large budget deficit and the reduction in tax revenues precipitated by the recession. But hope of a provincial solution to Toronto's government has not entirely disappeared. 'The candle still burns, waiting to be turned up again when a proportion of the political leadership agrees.'[31]

Passing verdict – disillusion overshadows Metro's achievements

The discussion of Metro among the cognoscenti in the 1990s focuses more on its failings than its achievements. Barlow posed the idea that metropolitan government, in any case, was going out of fashion in the 1980s.[32] People, politicians and bureaucrats in the city are more likely to talk about getting out of Metro than how it might be expanded. The City was incensed that its taxpayers were being asked in 1992, when its own revenues were hit by the decline in the occupation of downtown offices, to contribute more to Metro, and to schools. Demonstrators, mostly from small businesses, stormed the City Hall. The province stepped in to halt the proposed increases.

A plan for the re-arrangement of functions was being hatched by some City councillors, whereby the City would fund and manage education, pay Metro to continue the policing function and some other services, including social services, which would be taken over by the province in due course. Public transit would go to one overall authority instead of being shared by several bodies as it is now. The City does not necessarily question the quality of Metro services, but the cost of paying for two tiers of government is a handicap on business (Metro agrees that it charges business more steeply than residents).

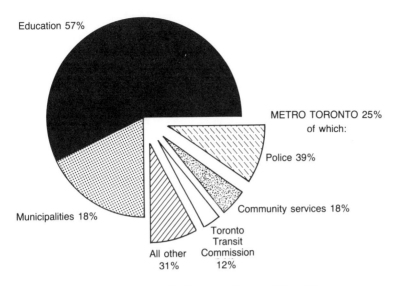

Education 57%

METRO TORONTO 25%
of which:

Police 39%

Community services 18%

Municipalities 18%

Toronto
Transit
All other Commission
31% 12%

Figure 5.7 How the property tax dollar is spent. *Source*: Metro Toronto.

The City is also worried that long overdue moves by the province to change the base for assessment of property for tax purposes, if implemented on the basis of current plans, will actually penalize occupants of older buildings in and around the centre, to the advantage of taxpayers in other parts of Metro. But it is not only the City which is increasingly uncomfortable with the current arrangements. Other municipalities are doing sums on what it would cost to provide services without Metro. Some of their constituents want government to be smaller and more responsive. The six municipalities in Metro, as much as Metro itself, are viewed as too remote and distant by some.

These rumblings of discontent need to be heard partly in the context of Canadians' complaint that they are 'over-governed' – four tiers of government for Metro Toronto, for instance (municipal, Metro, province, Federal) – and overlapping of functions. Metro receives less than half of its funding from Federal and provincial sources. Property taxes raise just under 40%, payments for services providing the balance. In contrast to Federal and provincial government, Metro, and the municipalities, including school boards, have reduced their debt over the last 20 years. Their debt charges as a percentage of revenues were down to 3% in 1990 from 17.8% in 1970.

Some services, however, call out to be organized on a territorial basis that is bigger than Metro. The expanded urban territory and growth in consumption has accelerated the need for new waste disposal sites to be identified. The province set up the Interim Waste Authority in 1991 to identify and develop disposal systems and sites for hazardous waste, for example, which had been handled in part by Metro (which had itself taken over the function from local councils in 1967).

The present difficulties need not detract from the achievements of the past. Indeed, so far as they prompt discussion and proposals, they indicate 'a willingness to sustain change'.[33] '. . . marks of its success are its very survival and the fact that there has never been any serious thought given to reverting to the pre-Metro situation'.[34] Don Stevenson, at the Canadian Urban Institute[35] believed, however, that 'much of what was good would have happened anyway because of the nature of governance in Canada, and particularly in Ontario'.

Avoiding the inner city trap

The institution of Metro, however, did help to avoid the wealth divisions between the suburbs, inner city and central city, and between minorities, which have dogged other cities. Metro 'provided for the ordered development of the suburbs'.[36]

> One of the reasons that the Metro Toronto region was able to manage its growth over the past several decades was because of good public institutions. These institutions were able to respond to the rapid growth and increasing diversity which has occurred during this last phase. Our role here as the processor of such a large number of immigrants has given us a special challenge. Metro gave us the ability to plan and act across the region in dealing with these problems.[37]

Schools were one example where the authority that comparatively well-paid teachers are given was of huge benefit in a city that was trying to create an identity among children with diverse ethnic backgrounds. Teachers' salaries came under fire in the 1990s, however, as the deficits in provincial and Federal budgets escalated and municipal government was juggling services to satisfy the demands of the powerful teachers' unions. Schools are funded by the Metro School Board, which equalizes the funding of schools across Metro, and takes into account special needs. Six elected school boards – one for each municipality – are responsible for overseeing day-to-day management of the schools.

Housing was another example. In the early days of Metro, the municipalities were asked to include low-cost housing in their plans. Although they were not bound legally to conform, they did make provision. Low-cost housing for rent and purchase is again in short supply, however. House prices escalated in the late 1980s. They dropped back, but were still out of reach of low-income earners. The average house price in 1993 in the GTA was C$200 000. Their choice is between high rents or social housing projects, provided by the province, and run by Metro. These projects suffer some of the familiar problems. 'Crack cocaine just blew us. It's aggressive. Marijuana was not aggressive. We now have guns.'[38]

Toronto avoided ghettos in which minority groups are dominant. There are concentrations of ethnic groups, but more on the scale of neighbourhoods than whole districts. New immigrants, who were arriving at the rate of 50 000 annually during the second half of the 1980s, are allocated to districts across the city. Population density within the Metro area is more akin to European than American cities. This has been partly responsible for the centre of the city still being lived in by the middle-classes. The

> older city displayed for the most part a strong immune system, so to speak . . . Canadian banks – unlike U.S. banks – did not adopt the practice of 'redlining' various city neighbourhoods, designating property in them to be ineligible henceforth, for mortgages or other financial infusions . . . old and modest Toronto neighbourhoods were not automatically doomed to destruction, preceded by enforced dilapidation and deterioration . . . These neighbourhoods are not exceptional in Toronto as in so many American cities; rather, they are the rule.[39]

This did not all happen without incident. One of the high spots of Toronto municipal history was the revolt in the late 1960s of disparate groups against the City Council's backing of neighbourhood clearances to make way for the developers, and to build new highways. In 1972, a new Council, headed by John Sewell, was elected to the city on pledges that it would not sanction clearances. The provincial government put expressway plans on hold, the clearances were halted. The neighbourhoods saved from the bulldozer were often gentrified. Districts like the 'Annexe' – saved from the proposed Spadina Expressway – and 'Cabbagetown', survived and strengthened.

Stability of government in the city has helped to bring about the distribution of diversity. Toronto's expanding economy in the 1980s both made it highly desirable for prospective immigrants, and was spurred with the infusion of new arrivals, often bringing capital and skills. Many like Toronto because it is a reasonably safe and harmonious city. The Hong Kong Chinese are the latest instance of people coming from countries where city living is the norm. Stable local government was a factor in attracting corporate investment to the city as well.

Metro Toronto's own assessment of its competitive position in relation to the GTA and Ontario, however, puts a question mark after 'governance' in listing its liabilities, while costs and taxes are definitely in this category. Taxes are also listed as a liability pitched against competition in the national and international arenas. Metro argues, however, that the problem is the 'artificial tax border', by which it means that it is making payments towards certain services beyond its boundaries, and therefore subsidizing those authorities which do not make any contribution.

5.4 ECONOMIC DEVELOPMENT

Natural resources and shipping

The original sources of Toronto's growth came from the minerals and timber in the hinterland. The town actually started as a centre of government in the newly colonized country. By the middle of the nineteenth century, it had blossomed into a commercial port which grew in parallel with its hinterland. Natural products were brought to Toronto to be transshipped for export to Europe, where they were much in demand. Concurrent with the development of Toronto as a port on the St Lawrence Seaway route was the growth of its own industry in and around the city. By the latter part of the nineteenth century, Toronto – now the third largest manufacturing area in North America – already had a significant industrial base.

State intervention was part of the process of stimulating development in the city. Federal and provincial government funded infrastructure, and fostered development in certain areas. Ownership and control of the entire waterfront was vested in the Toronto Harbour Commission, set up in 1911. The Commission had the authority to develop the area not merely as a harbour but for industrial and commercial uses. Much later, as industry on the waterfront declined, another public agency, the Harbourfront Corporation (a Crown Corporation) was given the authority to initiate a new role for the waterfront. Its results have not drawn widespread applause. Multi-storey apartment blocks in the 'luxury' price range have been much criticized on account of their exclusivity and physical presence in an area that had once been planned as public space. The compensating facilities for art and craft workshops, however, have been received much more favourably.

Financial services and communications

Another leg in the development of the city's economy stemmed from the trading in commodities, and banking and insurance, which built up by the second half of the last century, and which, much later, was to benefit from investment in a sophisticated system of communications in the region. Canada's switching network was scheduled to be entirely digitalized by 1994. The stimulus provided by private telecommunications service providers in Canada at the instigation of the government 'have led to demand side pressures to innovate almost unique in Canada'.[40] Toronto-based

Northern Telecom and Bell Canada supplied technologies and equipment, including digital switching systems, Common Channel Signalling and ISDN (Integrated Services Digital Network), which have enabled subscribers to choose from a range of 'intelligent' services built into the network. Toronto matched or exceeded leading cities in the US and 'most major financial centres in the world in terms of access lines with digital switching and advanced signalling technology'.[41] The city also claims that it has the largest free calling area on the North American continent.

Figure 5.8 Downtown Toronto: spending by the federal and provincial governments assisted city growth. *Courtesy of Metropolitan Toronto Convention and Visitors Association.*

The Toronto Stock Exchange (TSE) trades around half the volume of all shares in Canada. The value of shares traded in 1993 was a record C$140 billion. The TSE has also established its credentials in the rapidly growing sector of trading in options. The system of trading itself was scheduled to be fully automated by early 1994. The TSE focuses most of its attention on Canadian investors, however. 'Our general view at the moment is to concentrate our marketing on our existing products and try to improve their liquidity', said the president of the TSE, Mr Pearce Bunting, in 1992.[42]

Over the last decade, Toronto has consolidated its position as the lead banking centre in the country, overtaking Montreal. Three (Canadian Imperial Bank of Commerce, Bank of Nova Scotia, Toronto Dominion Bank) of the five major Canadian-based banks have their head offices in Toronto. The city has also scooped the pool of foreign banks setting up in the country – although the largest foreign bank in 1992, Hongkong Bank of Canada, had its headquarters in Vancouver – and securities dealers. (Canadian-based banks can own securities houses since deregulation of financial services in 1987.)

Between 45 and 50 foreign banks operate in the city, including Citibank, Credit Suisse, Barclays, Morgan Bank, and Swiss Bank Corp. of Canada, through to banks catering mostly for immigrant minorities. Foreign-owned banks have made little inroad on the domestic banks in retail banking. Toronto is also the major centre for life insurance companies, headed by Sun Life Assurance Co. of Canada, and other forms of insurance. About 178 000 people in the GTA were employed in the sector covering finance, insurance and real estate.

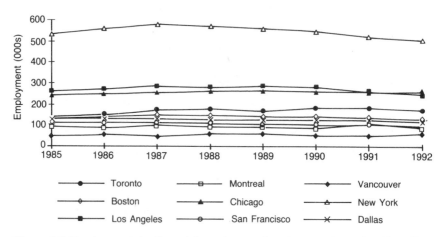

Figure 5.9 Employment in financial services and real estate in major Canadian and American cities, 1985–92. *Source*: US Dept of Labour, Statistics Canada, 1985–92.

The geographical hub of the sector is in Bay and King Streets. The skyline of Toronto spouted skyscrapers for the head offices of the big banks from the 1970s on, Royal Bank Plaza, First Canadian Place – the first of the Reichman brothers' major developments – to the 68-storey Bank of Nova Scotia, developed by Robert Campeau, who, like the Reichmanns, stumbled in the New York property market. The back offices of the banks and insurance companies, meanwhile, fan out around the city core, into the suburbs.

The prospering of support services

The services sector as a whole employs over 900 000, nearly three times the numbers in manufacturing. Fast-growing sub-sectors like industrial design, however, are often directly linked to manufacturing. After finance, insurance, and real estate, business services is the next biggest sector in services, followed by health and welfare. The biggest single employer, however, was the Ontario provincial government, located in Toronto. In total, some 5% of Toronto's workforce is in the government sector.

Services are significant not only in terms of employment, but also as inputs of goods exported. International trade in services as a singular entity has been growing but it still represents only about one-quarter of total international trade by value. However, 'relatively few industries in the Canadian services sector have reached international standing and Canada's service exports as a percentage of total exports are the lowest of the G7' countries.[43]

The slide in manufacturing employment

Measured in terms of jobs, manufacturing has declined steeply in the last decade. One-quarter of the Toronto region's (Census Metropolitan Area) workforce was employed in manufacturing in 1981. In 1992 it was down to less than a fifth (18.2%) after the massive restructuring in the early 1980s and 1990s. In electrical manufacturing, 10 000 jobs disappeared between 1990 and 1991. The axe fell particularly hard in the city. Jobs lost in manufacturing plants which closed down in the Metro area in 1993 were the most since the Economic Development Department had started to keep records, with new plants being built in the suburbs and further out. Restructuring was the answer to global pressure for lower cost products, accentuated by the 1989 free trade agreement between Canada and the United States. The elimination of bilateral tariff barriers in many traded goods and services would take ten years. Three years later, the North American Free Trade Agreement introduced Mexico as the third trading partner.

But it was not only manufacturing. Banks took the opportunity to cut their cost base. Some 6000 jobs also went in financial services between 1991 and 1992. The retail sector was hit badly. Unemployment went over 10% in 1991 and has not perceptibly improved since. Economists' concern is that other parts of Ontario, and the rest of the country have regained the levels of employment prior to the recession but the Toronto regional economy was still down by about 10% from its pre-recession peak employment level.[44]

The recession had not been anticipated even by the business community, and certainly not by the politicians. 'Toronto thought it was insulated against international trends. Almost overnight, market forces have predominated.'[45] 'It turned out that Toronto was at the epicentre of the recession.'[46] It was a chilling experience in a city accustomed to growth and a high standard of living for a quarter of a century, and never more so than in the second half of the 1980s when the services sector and real estate had swept it along on a wave of wealth. Food banks had to be set up, and were used by 140 000 a month at the height of the recession.

The exposure of the Toronto region to global pressures was exacerbated by the over-valued Canadian dollar, and high interest rates relative to the United States in the early 1990s, as well as the fall-out from the free trade agreement. The trading picture improved with the devaluation of the Canadian dollar and fall in interest rates. Between 1992 and 1993 the Canadian dollar dropped 8% against the American dollar. Economists are quick to point out that the free trade agreement has a positive side as well, with opportunities in the Mexican market, for instance, which are waiting to be exploited.

Despite its diminishing employment base, manufacturing remains a major source of employment in the Toronto region compared with other cities of similar size in North America, and a vibrant force in the economy. As a buyer of technical, legal and financial services it helps to maintain many more jobs.

More than 80% of the Canadian automotive industry is in south Ontario. Automotive exports by the province were 42% of the total in 1991, while imports were 22%. Transportation equipment, which includes vehicles, is also significant in Canadian manufactured exports. The big three Detroit-based manufacturers (General Motors, Ford, Chrysler) dominate, Japanese-based Honda and Toyota have also set up in the region. The industry has also been at the forefront of global rationalization, a process hastened by the free trade agreement prompting American-owned producers to re-examine the rationale for being located in Canada. But the removal of tariff barriers has also strengthened the region's bid to be an integral part of the Great Lakes automotive industry in North America, concentrating on fewer, highly modern plants. An example is the Chrysler assembly plant in Brampton, within the Toronto region, now one of the prime producers of Chrysler vans.

Some of the smaller manufacturing operations, however, set up in Canada originally simply to jump the tariff barrier, have skipped back over the border. Tax concessions offered in locations in the north of New York State, for instance, attracted between 200 and 300 Canadian firms from 1985 on.[47]

Metro Toronto's economists have refuted some of the criticims made by Harvard business strategist Michael Porter in his analysis of Canada's competitive position, for the Canadian government. They emphasize the comparative advantages that the GTA enjoys, for example, in a manufacturing workforce with some post-secondary education (Ontario: 44%, compared with southern states in the United States, where the proportion is less than 30%); and annual labour costs substantially lower than in the Detroit area.

But Toronto is losing the traditional industries which are highly sensitive to wage costs, including fashion and furniture-making, in favour of locations in the United States and Mexico. The clothing sector is responsible for about 14 000 jobs in Metro Toronto. Fashion is the largest industrial employer in the City of Toronto. The City's economic development arm has been engaged in a support programme to upgrade the industry and thereby secure a more certain future. The city's group of fashion designers are promoted in the United States as well as Canada, workspace and shared manufacturing facilities have been made available. The ups and downs of the industry are a reminder of the importance of small, independent producers in the city economy, the possibilities of strengthening a traditional industry, but also of the underlying competitive threats from cheaper locations.

Capitalizing on free trade

Toronto is actively marketing itself to European and Pacific Rim companies as a regional base for the North American market with the disappearance of the border barrier. The city cannot offer tax incentives as attractive as American cities, but it uses other ploys: it is more export-oriented – 'The Americans talk about free trade, but they act differently', remarked one economist; and it vigorously promotes its qualities like communications, public transit, arts, choice of housing, etc. More important in the competitive game between cities is that it can genuinely parade its 'quality of life', in public education and healthcare, and the low crime rate – in 1990, Toronto suffered 1.9 murders per 100 000 population against 30.7 in New York City, and 34.8 in Houston.

Toronto is a head office city. In 1992, according to the local *Business Magazine*, it claimed the head offices of over half of Canada's top 50 private sector companies (by revenues). General Motors of Canada topped the list, followed by Sun Life Assurance, Manufacturers' Life Insurance,

Confederation Life Insurance and IBM Canada. The Greater Toronto area had more corporate head offices than any metropolitan area in North America, according to research conducted by Metro's economic staff who applied an adjusted exchange rate between the United States and Canada to arrive at what they claim is a more accurate reading of the North American Fortune 500 Industrials List. New York City was next on the headquarters list.[48] Toronto's strengths currently, however, are essentially national in head office terms rather than international.

5.5 SOCIAL DEVELOPMENT

Fragile future for a globally respected system

The Canadian system of public education, healthcare, care for the disadvantaged is admired worldwide. But Canada's Liberal government, elected in 1993, has given warning that in restoring the Federal and provincial budget deficits to some sort of normality, everything has to be examined. A total review of the financing of the welfare state was announced. The Government's first budget in winter 1994 was slanted towards the encouragement of business expansion, with cuts in unemployment insurance premiums paid by employers, for example.

The war on public spending spells certain squeezes on cities although for Toronto, which had enjoyed 'the highest standard of public services in North America, and all delivered by Conservative governments in Ottawa',[49] the cuts have not been as severe as had been anticipated.

The Metro government distributes welfare payments on behalf of the government, and must contribute 20% of the total. With progressively more rigorous requirements in qualifying for unemployment pay, demand for welfare has soared. In 1993, for example, out of between 220 000 and 230 000 people who registered as out of work, only 135 000, in one month, were claiming unemployment pay.

Pockets of poverty exist in the city. Tensions between the black population in particular and the police have been raised at times. Canada's policy on immigrants has always been selective, but the country has a rising number of refugees, and people claiming refugee status, who do not have the same rights as immigrants. Some of the most disadvantaged in the Toronto area are native Indians.

For many immigrants, Canada still is 'a wonderful place', as a Sri Lankan doctor put it in spring 1992. He was attending a course designed to help new arrivals bringing often professional skills to get on the bottom rung of the employment ladder. They learn, for instance, to adapt their accented English more closely to Canadian English.

Community development in the city has tended to be downgraded to a single social need.

We didn't realise that it is community-based organizations that spawn local leadership and local citizenship. We now know that funding of local community organizations is critical. They need core funding, not just project funding.[50]

The suburban authorities frequently have made poor provision for community needs. In Scarborough – dubbed by social workers as 'the place from which everybody wants to escape' – the gap between facilities created by developers for profit and the paucity of community accommodation is surprising in a city which prides itself on its social support. Young people are particularly poorly catered for, according to social workers. They cite examples of young people being hounded out by shopping mall managers who tolerate older people not spending money.

A family resource centre in an immigrant area of North York was started by second-generation Italian women, out of sheer need for relief from loneliness in the vast suburbs. It flourished, with an impressive array of people – old, young, encompassing six languages. 'It is part of being Canadian to know one's neighbours', said an elderly Korean lady, who was taking part in the proceedings courtesy of a young Korean mother conducting the translations. But, in 1992, the modest funding from Metro and United Way (which channels charitable donations to good causes) was cut, and accommodation for the group was uncertain.

So Toronto is confronted with a trace of social and racial tensions common in American cities: youth unemployment and older, low-skilled workers made redundant from closed plants. And a new class is emerging of single parents who cannot participate in the economy. Whereas the disadvantaged once stemmed out of recent immigrant groups, who had moved up the economic scale at least within a generation, they are now unrelated to ethnic background.

'The first ring of suburbs (the Scarboroughs and North Yorks) will be the place where decline may occur and the poor congregate'; 'My areas have good mixtures of ethnic groups and there are few problems. They are more ones of class than race. Downtown Toronto community services are given more support to make social housing work. It is the suburbs that are in need.'[51]

Where does Toronto go now?

Government in Toronto has had few critics among the general public and the business community until recently. True, there were vigorous protests over the city's various redevelopment plans over 20 years ago, and of the downtown skyline mirroring dozens of American cities, and of missed opportunities in exploiting the waterfront. But, at the level of service provision, it had been held generally as reasonably efficient.

But business, government and public services have all come under more scrutiny as the implications of the international corporate adjustment to competitive pressures and lowering of trade barriers began to be appreciated. What Porter titled 'the comfortable insularity of the old order' in his study of Canadian competitiveness was well and truly tested in the early 1990s, and particularly in Toronto which has a relatively high dependency on manufacturing.

Porter, in the 1991, study emphasized some of the weaknesses that Canadian business had been able to overlook for a long time, particularly poor vocational training provision, low rate of innovation in business, over-dependence on finished products in manufacturing sectors, and lack of rivalry in the domestic market (telecommunications was one exception). Solutions mostly lie outside the scope of local government. Porter emphasized, in any case, that it is companies which must change.

The Toronto business scene is changing. There is a shift away from European markets, particularly Britain, to the United States, and renewed interest among American companies in tapping into the underlying potential of Canadian companies. Canadian business, unlike big American corporations, has not tended to strike partnerships with the public sector in the education and social arenas. With the growing American slant to business, and government pressure on resources for funding public services, more American style solutions might emerge. The city's bid for the 1996 Olympic Games did not demonstrate the sort of support from all quarters which helped to win the Games for Atlanta.

Business in Toronto is beginning to find its voice, stung into action by some of the province's programmes which business construed as antagonistic to its interests. The Toronto Board of Trade called for 'a fundamental re-think of the welfare safety net. On education, business pays for over half the education costs, but it is going into pots which are not accountable. We are not getting value for money.'[52] There have been some responses to business lobbying. The Ontario Training and Adjustment Board has been set up by the province as an independent, self-governing body which brings together employers and providers of government-funded training programmes to sharpen up the relevance of the programmes towards employers' requirements.

At the City level, modest economic development projects are being funded by government: promoting contacts between research institutes and pharmaceutical companies at regular meetings to which financial advisers and specialists in intellectual property law are sometimes invited in a bid to strengthen the biomedical base in the city – 'The real success will be when we see lots of small companies coming out of the initiative';[53] international filmmakers are using the city and developing an industry which had its roots in the government's film board, taking advantage of Toronto's 'safe city' image and pleasant suburban streets for filming; tourism, particularly from the United States, has been boosted by attractive hotel prices since the exchange rate was adjusted and off-Broadway shows in the safe downtown.

Toronto's international appeal has been hugely enhanced in the past two decades, the arts scene being particularly strong in cinema, theatre and visual arts. The province's art gallery in the city has been refurbished and expanded with great care, and the city has a cluster of private art galleries. A new conductor was taking over the Toronto symphony orchestra in 1994. Plans for a new opera house had been resurrected, albeit on a more modest scale than the earlier plans. But, if it comes off, it looked like being due to an interesting mix of funding from the public and private sectors being arranged.

NOTES

1. Stein, D. L. (1993) *Going Downtown*, Oberon Press, Canada.
2. Ibid.
3. *The Composition and Implications of Metropolitan Toronto's Ethnic, Racial and Linguistic Populations* (1990) Metro Toronto.
4. Blumenfeld, H. (1974) Public policy and the future urban system, *Urban Futures for Central Canada*, University of Toronto Press.
5. Barlow, I. M. (1991) *Metropolitan Government*, Routledge.
6. Jacobs, J. (1993) Foreword in J. Sewell, *The Shape of the City*, University of Toronto Press.
7. *Municipal Government in the GTA* (1992) Urban Focus Series 92–8, Canadian Urban Institute.
8. Interview with the author, February 1994.
9. *Disentanglement in Several Jurisdictions – Comparison with Ontario* (1992) Canadian Urban Institute.
10. Interview with the author, February 1994.
11. *Urban Structures Concepts Study* (1990) Summary Report, IBI Group.
12. *Decisions and Recommendations of the Board* (1953) The Ontario Municipal Board (Cumming Report).
13. Barlow, *Metropolitan Government, op. cit.*
14. Cumming Report, *op. cit.*
15. Ibid.
16. Ibid.
17. Ibid.
18. Barlow, *Metropolitan Government, op. cit.*
19. Cumming Report, *op. cit.*
20. Cumming, L. (1958) *Metropolitan Toronto Commission of Inquiry.*
21. Church, G. in interview with the author, February 1994
22. Barlow, *Metropolitan Government, op. cit.*
23. Ibid.
24. Ibid.
25. Ibid.

26. *Disentanglement in Several Jurisdictions, op. cit.*
27. *Municipal Government in the GTA* (1992) Canadian Urban Institute.
28. *Municipal Government in the Toronto Region* (1992) Canadian Urban Institute.
29. Sewell, J. (1993) *The Shape of the City*, University of Toronto Press.
30. Ibid.
31. Church, G, in interview with the author, February 1994.
32. Barlow, *Metropolitan Government, op. cit.*
33. Church, G, in interview with the author, February 1994.
34. Barlow, *Metropolitan Government, op. cit.*
35. Interview with the author, February 1994.
36. Gilbert, R. and Stevenson, D., Canadian Urban Institute, in interview with the author, February 1994.
37. Novick, M, then Dean, Community Services, Ryerson Polytechnical Institute, former director of Metro Toronto's Social Planning Council, in interview with German-Marshall Fund team, April 1992.
38. Benton, Clive, director, Jane-Finch Community Centre, in interview with the German-Marshall Fund team, April 1992.
39. Jacobs, *The Shape of the City, op. cit.*
40. Porter, M. (1991) *Canada at the Crossroads*, a study prepared for the Business Council on National Issues and the Government of Canada.
41. City of Toronto promotion brochure.
42. *Financial Times*, 23 February 1993.
43. Porter, *Canada at the Crossraods, op. cit.*
44. Metro EDD Research Group (1993) *Year End Review*.
45. Tonks, A., Chairman of Metro Toronto, in interview with German-Marshall Fund Team, April 1992.
46. Donald M. Baxter, executive director, Economic Development, Metro Toronto, in interview with the author, February 1994.
47. *Financial Times*, 23 February 1993.
48. *Economic Information Bulletin of Metro Toronto*, August 1993.
49. Novick, M, in interview with the author, February 1994.
50. Novick, M, in interview with German-Marshall Fund Team, April 1992.
51. Metro Councillors Brian Ashton and Joan King, in interviews with the German-Marshall Fund team, April 1992.
52. Don King, then President Toronto Board of Trade, in interview with the German-Marshall Fund team, April 1992.
53. Bob McArthur, Economic Development Officer, City of Toronto, in interview with the author, February 1994.

Conclusions 6

6.1 OBITUARIES ARE OUT OF PLACE

Four cities, four countries in two continents, a study undertaken when
each was in recession, and then expanded when the western economies
were recovering. In 1992, the business climate in the cities was depressed:
industrial plants closing, banks shedding workers, shopping centres
denuded of customers and retailers. The only abundance was in signs
indicating property to let. Two years later, the signs were of business confidence returning: new tenants were moving into offices, job advertise-
ment columns in newspapers expanding, contractors moving on to vacant
sites.

Some cities proved more durable than many dared to hope at the low
point of the recession. There is nothing new in this. Time and again, it
has been assumed that the economic role of cities in the wider community
has been on the point of diminishing – in the 1960s in the United States,
the 1970s in Britain, the 1980s in western Europe, the 1990s in eastern
Europe. In most cases, they have survived, and some have even started to
expand after a long period of decline. It was the suburbs, and smaller
cities and towns with a high dependency on big employers, particularly in
high-technology industries and services, which fared worse in the early
1990s recession. For cities, that recession was a replay.

All the same, the prolonged economic downturn was serious. Plans to
inject new life into run-down parts of cities had to be dropped or at best
modified. Unemployment has come down in some cities, but the proportion who have been out of work for six months and more is higher. Most
worrying is that the numbers not working in poor areas can be seen to
vary little between recession and recovery. With unemployment in double
digits, companies going out of business and shrinking tax revenues, cities
received little compensation from their governments. For their part, governments determined that spending on social support mechanisms –
running as high as 14% of gross domestic product – should not under-

mine their goal of restoring balance to national budgets. Having already abandoned their commitment to full employment, the politicians were planning to pull away from providing the secure safety net of welfare.

6.2 DIVIDED THEY STAND

The moral of the recession, the second in a decade for many countries, is that the future of cities lies in their ability to stimulate their existing resources. That said, cities will always depend on the higher levels of government for a part of the money which they spend on services and, indeed, to finance major transport projects. American city mayors want more than this, however. Kurt Schmoke of Baltimore argued that what is needed is

> a national policy to rejuvenate cities. State and local government can do more . . . But none of this alone, or together, can substitute for a national government that recognizes its own self-interest in helping cities, and its moral obligation to the millions of its citizens who live in cities.[1]

Europe and Canada present a different picture. The scale of neighbourhood deterioration is nothing like as great as in the cities of the United States. The Americans say that, in part, this is because, in European cities, there is an effective safety net for the disadvantaged. But the strings of this net are fraying. In any case there are other factors. The French government in particular looks on its cities as economic 'engines of growth' – although they also have many problem areas – and has invested in major infrastructure projects to help them compete for business. The province of Ontario similarly supported a long period of growth in Toronto. Cities in the European Union, hit hard by industrial contraction in the early 1980s, have had access to an additional source of finance, although European funds are tied more closely to regional development than to urban problems.

Meanwhile, the deep divisions in many American cities are becoming more evident in Europe and Canada. They are not always about money. As an example, over 30% of children leave school in Canada – one of the most well-funded systems of education in the western world – without any qualification. Very often, they are simply not interested in school. European and Canadian schools are only slowly implementing the sort of links long ago developed between American schools, business and institutions of higher education, which can, with much patient work, help to motivate children to stay in school. Mentoring of potential problem children by volunteers is also common in the United States.

Business will be the basic source of wealth in cities. City governments are having to concentrate on the core job of providing services. The sort of innovative public-sector projects designed to diversify the city economy in the 1980s will be progressively curtailed by public spending priorities in the 1990s. What the authorities must do is provide the basic blocks on which the business sector can build. There is a lengthy list.

They must ensure that young people are educated to the stage where they can learn relevant skills and provide the training in vocational skills that will be more in demand as employers concentrate more on adding value to their products. They must be more environmentally alert: cities need to be cleaner, friendlier, and more visually stimulating. They must encourage the economic and social participation of ethnic minorities, people with learning difficulties, the elderly and the long-term unemployed. Politicians and officials must show that they can work with their counterparts in areas outside the city to devise plans for dealing effectively with the needs of business and citizens.

To achieve these goals, cities can learn from each other. Each study in this book highlighted one episode in the history of the city in detail: business and political alliance in Atlanta, economic development in Birmingham, land-use planning in Rotterdam and governance in Toronto. No one element can be isolated, however. Each must relate to the totality of the city.

The first chapter of the book pointed to what cities had experienced in common. Job losses in manufacturing were an inevitable consequence of the realignment in location by companies serving international markets. Middle-class families and business left behind the constraints imposed by the city, and went to the suburbs. They were replaced by immigrants, mostly from the poorer and politically unstable parts of the globe. All this happened within a relatively short space of time.

This concluding chapter pulls out ideas that might be adapted by cities wanting to sustain a successful economy. To be successful, cities have to maximize their advantages in the face of the attractions of suburban development. They cannot afford to be complacent. Like the economy, they have to be constantly adapting and adding value. This cannot be left, however, wholly to officials and their political masters in the city hall. Cities are made up of an array of sectoral interests over which there is no structure of command. The sectors are independent of each other. The formal means through which co-ordination can be achieved are weak. Therefore 'informal arrangements to promote co-operation are especially useful. These informal modes of co-ordinating efforts across institutional bundaries are what I call "civic co-operation".'[2]

Stone, whose specific study was of Atlanta, emphasized the importance of business within this scheme, not to the exclusion of other interests like churches, trade unions, but because 'the economic role of businesses and the resources they control are too important for these enterprises to be left out completely'. Sometimes, the initiative to promote informal arrangements for co-operation comes from the private sector. But in European and Canadian cities, the impetus is more likely to come from the elected politicians. They must broker effective partnerships between, for example, business, education, the community. At the same time politicians need to acquire greater sensitivity towards small and medium-sized companies. In the past, planners have hindered such firms by squeezing them out of areas of mixed use.

6.3 DONATION AND SUPPLICATION

In fact, politicians and officials everywhere have a natural tendency to create bureaucracies and fiefdoms which become remote from the people they are supposed to serve. The same could be said of businesses in the past. But few employers can afford to be out of touch today with their customers.

It is true that local administration has to perform a more delicate balancing act between those who provide its finance and its customers, the residents, than does business. But national governments, the ultimate source of control, are inconsistent, wanting a tighter rein on local finance, while loosening the leash when it suits them. Studies have been done on both sides of the Atlantic putting the case for cities to be treated more by their governments on the French pattern, as 'engines of growth', rather than as supplicants. Cities – Paris is an obvious example, but so too is Toronto – which have been viewed positively by government have generally prospered. But mostly this lobbying has had little impact on politicians who hand out money – never enough, say the cities – to alleviate social problems.

When a city slides into deep economic difficulties, the response has tended towards giving grants to companies or tax rebates to individuals who invest. But the value of these handouts can be swamped when politicians postpone decisions on infrastructure, for example, which would be much more to the longer term benefit of a city's competitive position.

The gap between the money from government and what is needed to provide local services is made up from local taxation. The local authorities have the leeway to innovate only when they have a source of additional revenue, say, from an airport (Atlanta) or port (Rotterdam) or exhibition centre (Birmingham). The constraints on what local government can spend and levy tightened in Britian after Mrs Margaret Thatcher won the 1983 election. But the other sanction is the level of tax which can be obtained before business and people look for lower taxed areas into which they might move.

The main function of local government, as it is perceived at the centre, is to provide services to the public. These usually include education, both schools and adult education. In some cases they provide water and sewerage facilities, social services, housing, highways, refuse collection and waste disposal. They provide these services directly, or contract them out to the private sector. Even a few schools are being contracted out under pilot projects, like that in Baltimore.

6.4 ARRANGED MARRIAGES

Within this functional emphasis of local government, the relationship between local and central, state and provincial government is changing. Decision-making and administrative powers of local government in Britain have been diluted by the Conservative government. Rather than pass the money down to local politicians to decide how to use it, the centre decided that it knew best. So responsibility is sometimes transferred downwards, bypassing local government, while financial controls at the centre are stronger. Partnering business is now required in certain areas.

Housing is an example of how local political power is diffusing, how local authorities are being pushed into new relations, sometimes with their constitutents, sometimes with new official bodies, but in any case into new partnerships. Most big cities have large areas of public housing built from the 1930s onwards. This housing has been not only a source of power – people in public housing were far more dependent on their councils than home owners – but also, as time went on, a financial embarrassment, since the housing often required extensive repairs beyond the resources of the authority to carry out.

The British government found a popular policy solution: municipal authorities would offer their housing to tenants for purchase at a discount – the right-to-buy. As many as three million homes were sold. But inevitably it was the superior properties which went to private ownership, leaving councils with a rump of difficult properties. Now, large estates of problem housing are being transferred to trusts which are financed directly by central government for a period when some will be demolished and others refurbished. Tenants will decide at the end of the period if they want to go back to the local authority as landlord, or transfer to a housing association formed for the purpose.

On other estates, responsibility for managing repairs and maintenance is being transferred away from city housing departments to estate (tenant-controlled) management boards. The tenants are made to feel that they have a stake in their properties which they did not have under the old system of municipal management.

\

The Dutch government's approach is different. It has legislated for the housing owned by the municipalities to be transferred to housing associations. These are non-profit-making bodies, which have played the lead role in providing city housing for nearly a century. Many of the associations are very large, managing thousands of dwellings, but dependent on government support. That is now changing. They are being groomed to operate without government strings and subsidies except in providing housing for people with special needs. The planning of housing to cater for these needs is done in conjunction with the city authorities.

At the other end of the income scale, housing associations will be encouraged to provide rented accommodation in the range of middle incomes. But each example shows how the power that large housing portfolios had invested in local councils is being diffused. Some city programmes in the Netherlands, meanwhile, are experiments to give local neighbourhood committees the opportunity to top up certain services, as they choose.

In education, the notion of partnership is conceived differently. American city schools are experimenting with new governing bodies drawn from big corporations, business groups and parents, in an attempt to reverse worrying and deteriorating education standards. Pressure is being put on School Boards by business to reform faster. Schools in Britain have governing boards on which parents and local business are represented. They have the option of transferring the source of funding from local education authorities to the central education department. In both cases the power of the local authorities is being reduced in favour of new relationships, new partnerships.

Similarly, with training, old patterns of organization have been questioned. Employers viewed government-funded training in Britain, Canada, the Netherlands and the United States as a disaster. Training was generally of poor quality and frequently bore little relevance to what employers wanted. In the last few years, local boards drawn from employers (they must be in the majority on the Training and Enterprise Councils in Britain, whose origins lie in the longer-established Private Industry Councils in the United States) are attempting to devise a policy on local training which is linked to economic development. Such moves push local authorities into the role of either passive observer or simple administrator of programmes, the design of which has passed into other hands.

On the other hand, far from being passive, city councils are sometimes actively seeking to bring private and voluntary interests into sharing some of the traditional but growing burden imposed by social and educational difficulties. American cities have a head start, in that politicians and big businesses are more at ease about how they support each other. The Atlanta connection is an example: business leaders have even been used as negotiators in highly delicate political situtations. Budding players in

American local politics have in the past also depended on local property developers and contractors to support their election campaigns.

But the links between politicians and business are not exclusive to the United States. After witnessing the comings and goings of Toronto politicians over many years, one journalist concluded that 'for the more cynical, the people who believe that the true metaphor for our society is the market place', in local as well as in national politics 'a political decision means only that the politicians have received something in exchange for their votes'.[3]

It was the consortium of private-sector backers, including business, which strengthened the hand of Rotterdam's then chief planner in getting political backing for ambitious new development plans.[4] Birmingham has set up formal partnerships with business and representative bodies of commerce both in training and in the promotion of the city to potential investors. In the past, however, it was the informal, unpublicized agreements with business and developers which had a major influence on the physical development of the city.

Governments in Europe have picked up the American programme, originating in Boston, of formal compacts between schools and business which encourage teenagers to stay in school until leaving age. But the partnerships are not uniformly effective. The part played by big business – it is normally the large corporations which are active – in the social and educational arena of the United States sometimes has more of a 'feel-good' factor for the companies about it than benefits for the schools and neighbourhoods.

The Atlanta arrangements partnering schools and companies were found by the Chamber of Commerce to be very patchy in their impact. This is one reason why the progress of The Atlanta Project, launched by former President Jimmy Carter, and thereby almost automatically commanding a lot of publicity, will be closely examined. The Project leader insists that the chief executives of the big businesses supporting the Project meet once a month in person to keep up their interest as well as their money.

The motives of business executives in committing themselves to raising the achievement levels in poor schools must be recognized for what they are in part: economic self-interest. The skill of school principals seeking business support, and, indeed, of responsive corporate executives, is not to disguise this motive but to turn it to advantage. The goal is more difficult to realize where sustained commitment by business is sought to address social problems. But when a company can tailor its community effort to fit an identified interest of its own, the long-term results can be better for everybody than the unplanned response to the emotional call for help.

The British business sector no longer sees its contributions as purely philanthropic. But in Rotterdam, when the politicians sought business volunteers to help find solutions, the reaction reflected confusion, even distrust of politicians. In the Netherlands, as in Germany and other European states with highly organized social security structures, the tradition is that business pays government to provide for the needy, while companies get on with what they are good at. American cities, meanwhile, have more entrenched social deprivation. But some also have human resources in the voluntary sector and financial support from the charitable foundations not matched in European and Canadian cities. Students and retired people from the multitude of churches in Atlanta, for instance, help hard-pressed teaching staff by tutoring children with disadvantaged backgrounds.

6.5 CONTROL AND CONFUSION

The tradition of the state as the source of help in case of need is deeply rooted in European and Canadian culture, but is under strain from international and internal political pressure on governments to contain their public spending. In the Netherlands, which, like Britain, is a unitary state, most of the finance for services provided by local government comes from the centre which ties the provision of the finance to a service. In Canada, the key relationship is between city and province. In the United States, it is between city and state government, although there have been periods of Federal government intervention since World War II; this is being revived, although in more restricted fashion than in the 1960s, by the Clinton administration.

Local government boundaries in Canada and the United States can only be changed with the agreement of the province or state. Despite the physical expansion of cities like Atlanta and Toronto since the 1950s, their boundaries have not been widened. Britain introduced metropolitan government for the first time outside London in the early 1970s, then abandoned it in favour of single-tier authorities in the big cities. The Dutch government, on the other hand, is setting up metropolitan government for Rotterdam and other cities.

Good governance, however, is not only a matter of boundaries. The arguments favouring geographical limits which extend to the sphere of influence of the city proper still hold sway among local government watchers. In Rotterdam and other Dutch cities, a new metropolitan government is being formed partly after pressure was put on the government by the City. Politicians elsewhere might prefer the boundaries to stay where they are. Extending them brings in more of the middle class and probably shifts the balance of political power.

A more important issue than the definition of boundaries is the size of the local government tax base and the existence of arrangements to resolve anomalies between one authority and another. Companies do not normally move out of one area into another simply because of local tax rates, but it is a factor. If rates of tax did not differ so much and there was some system of equalization of revenues, deep divisions between rich and poor, particularly, in American cities, might lessen. Metropolitan government in Toronto is charged with setting a standard in services, particularly education, across the city and suburbs. But in most big American cities, the core city contains only a quarter of the metropolitan population, it has the largest concentrations of people on low incomes, yet no compensating support from the suburbs.

Large local authorities can be out of touch with their electorates. Two examples. Birmingham City Council planned to widen main roads into and out of the south side of the city in 1991–92. For business interests and commuters, the plans made sense, but they ignored the fact that local residents in the city did not want faster roads carving up their high street shopping. In Rotterdam, aldermen, who thought they knew their electorate, were surprised at the volley of criticisms which confronted them when they took themselves out to the people. They wanted to explain what they were doing. They found themselves having to defend, and cajole. By contrast, in Markham, a smaller, but fast developing suburb outside Toronto with a mainly middle-class population, the authorities are having to work hard in explaining to residents that by opposing more medium- and high-density developments, they will lose in the long term.

The idea that government gets closer to the people following a boundary change or the creation of a new tier of government is probably wishful thinking. The majority of the electorate typically does not bother to vote in American or British cities. The council of Metro Toronto, held by many observers to be one of the most efficient and responsive authorities, was not even elected by the public until 1988.

Meanwhile, business taxpayers, particularly small companies, frequently feel most alienated from local government. One solution to this problem is to bring in a wider cross-section of the community in planning for the future. The Atlanta Regional Commission – which is not elected and has no binding powers – wants to pin the regional planning process on the widest constituency of interests in the hope that those involved will identify the plans as their own and have the determination to see that they are implemented by the statutory authorities.

6.6 REDISCOVERING THE RESIDENTS

The idea of power being put in the hands of people to help themselves is catching. It is often referred to as 'empowerment', which originally meant giving political power to the black population in the United States. Now, it is used in management circles as well as in politics. Of course, it can be a fig leaf for politicians setting out first to cut support and, second, to transfer responsibility.

Cutting dependency has become a common cry among western governments. But there are harsh implications for cities where the proportion of the population dependent on state support is highest, unless it is handled with understanding. If it is to be done, it has to be done at the local level with a degree of flexibility which recognizes that no single type of agency is the perfect instrument. Settling what is suitable has to be worked out in the area in question. Arguably the failure always to do this limited the impact that the Federal programme, Model Cities, ought to have had, given its resources.

There is a surprising degree of consensus across the political divide that dependency is bad for both recipients and taxpayers. The more positive side, as it has emerged in Federal programmes in Canada and the United States, is the linking of unemployment pay and benefits in schemes which get people into work.

There is also an element here of building up the family as the unit which controls as well as looks after children. Parents are told that crime cannot always be excused because of poverty. It is up to them to keep their children out of crime. Senator Bill Bradley sought in 1992 'to bolster families in urban America' as a means of coming to terms with both crime and social anomalies. He was talking particularly about his own black community.[5] Rotterdam's liberal coalition city government experimented with 'Social Innovation', a policy to make people accept that they have duties where once they talked only of rights, which has been incorporated into the local government structure.

The disdvantaged need help if they are to be expected to take more control over their lives. Community development is a counterpart to tossing them out to fend for themselves. Given that city and town halls have sacrificed whole communities in the past to their plans, there is suspicion as well as apathy among people.

> People have to be persuaded to trust the change agents – and to become change agents themselves. They must define their own problems, establish their own priorities and take back the institutions that control their lives. People do not do such things if they are overwhelmed by feelings of powerlessness, as many of the people in our cities are.[6]

How a sense of community can be fostered will vary even from one neighbourhood to another. And the creation of it will be a long haul which will sometimes suffer reverses. Voluntary organizations can be very important. There are, however, some common threads. John Gardner, one of the most respected writers on community and leadership, pointed out that some sociologists thought 'they were witnessing the final disintegration of community' in American cities 40 years ago. 'But later studies have revealed that the capacity of communities to survive or reappear in altered form had been considerably underestimated.'[7]

He defined 'community' around the themes of: wholeness incorporating diversity; a reasonable base for shared values; caring, trust and teamwork; effective internal communication; participation; affirmation; links beyond the community; and development of young people.

Ronald Grzywinski, founder of the much admired South Shore Bank in Chicago, which has been described as 'a community development corporation with a bank', listed three key elements to develop community. First, the mechanism must be created for releasing the energies of local residents, since they will contribute most of the necessary work and talent. Second, the development institutions must control the resources needed for a comprehensive development programme and, third, the institution and the process must be self-sustaining and not depend on unreliable funding from government or foundations.

Some American cities have powerful community development corporations which can incorporate economic development with housing and social functions within a neighbourhood. City councils have worked increasingly with them over the last decade to help build up decaying areas. One important source of financial assistance to community-based initiatives is the Local Initiatives Support Corporation. Launched with core finance by the Ford Foundation, it leveraged this up mainly from institutions, which are able to claim tax rebates and therefore charge interest rates below the open market rates. The money is then parcelled out in grants and loans for housing and workspace developments.

The concept of neighbourhood economic development, spearheaded by local groups, is not unique to the United States. Community-based housing associations in Glasgow, for instance, have spawned economic development and training. The value of this approach is that it avoids the widespread process of large-scale clearance of declining property, undertaken by public authorities or at least with their backing, in favour of new building. This is then frequently occupied by newcomers at the expense of the original residents.

6.7 PEOPLE PERFORMANCE

Where a community group movement has been earmarked for attention from the top, its future is assured at least for a few years. But arguments fester about the impact of funding from the top on groups which have

grown out of the bottom. And there is another snare awaiting the unin-
itiated. The vulnerability of community group funding lies not only in
cuts by governments and charities. During the 1980s, private-sector style
performance measurement hit the public sector, so that recipients of
public finance are expected similarly to account for themselves by specify-
ing the outputs that they expect will result from the funded projects.
Government in Britain has probably gone furthest down this route, and
added another twist. Money for community groups operating in cities
now comes through programmes which are tightly defined by geographical area. The local authority must devise regeneration plans for
these districts, made up of schemes complete with projected outputs.

> How much easier to bid for schemes whose outputs can be measured
> in tonnes of concrete, numbers of successful graduates on training
> programmes or the leverage of private sector money, than those
> whose outcomes are more resilient communities or the release of local
> enterprise.[8]

Community groups in the United States have learned valuable lessons
from business. Under the auspices of The Atlanta Project, big companies
lend managers to groom community leaders in the neighbourhoods so
that they make proper use and account for the money allocated to them
from the centre. Professionalism in this sense is welcome. But care should
also be taken to help leaders devise targets which are realistic. There is
not much that even a well-managed project can do which will have an
impact in reducing the incidence of teenage pregnancies in a neighbourhood, since there are so many other social factors involved. Donors also
should be realistic in the returns which they expect.

The most devastating threat of all to community work, however, lies in
the effects of the drug culture on whole neighbourhoods. This is the
lesson from American cities, where even long-standing successes, like
South Shore, are finding that painstaking restoration of the neighbourhood is undermined by the impact of drugs, and particularly crack-
cocaine, on the residents. Crime rates which ballooned on the back of
drugs in public housing projects led to drastic measures, known as 'search
and sweep', to expel the affected families. Landlords refuse to rent apartments to families which include black teenage boys because so many
become implicated in drug-dealing.

Although less dramatically implemented in Europe, pockets of criminal
activities on housing estates have been similarly attacked by some authorities. The increase in drug abuse and crime is worst for the affected
neighbourhoods. If unchecked, however, a reputation is created which
can have an impact on the whole city, negating efforts to attract outside
investment in the form of business tourism and head offices.

6.8 COMMERCE AT LARGE

The underlying prosperity of the city depends on the competitiveness of its commerce, industry and institutions. Ask a chief executive of a size-able corporation how local government can help in keeping a company competitive and he may well be puzzled. He operates in a much larger world than that bounded by the city and its region. He probably lives outside the city, in an affluent suburb or smaller settlement many more miles on. He travels by car, which is parked in a secure place under his office building. His children do not attend city schools. If he participates in activities in the city, it is most likely in gatherings arranged by his pro-fessional association or a business representative group to which the company belongs. He might have noticed if new office blocks have gone up, that the streets in the centre have been made fit for pedestrians, that the city has sprouted a new theatre.

Or he might not, since his main concern about his company location is that he can get to an airport in less than an hour from where he can board a flight for another city, another continent, and that he does not get choked in traffic jams on his way home. Those criteria can be more easily met in locations out of the city. He might, however, be alerted to the fact that all is not well, when the personnel director reports that the company's testing of job applicants reveals that even school-leavers with qualifications come unprepared to be trained in basic skills; when mes-sages filter up to him that staff feel threatened in the streets even in the middle of the day; or that the chosen applicant for a high-level job has turned it down because he has decided not to move to what he considers a poor environment.

Economic development in the broadest sense requires, quite simply, that the city holds on to the companies that it has already, by making sure that the conditions are favourable enough for them to want to stay. It seems obvious, but, in fact, city authorities frequently put more of their effort into the less predictable, highly competitive business of attracting new companies. Existing satisfied customers are also the best advertise-ment in attracting new custom. The Chamber of Commerce in Atlanta and local authorities have capitalized on the companies that have moved to the region – most have located outside the city proper – by parading them in front of prospective incomers.

The ball does not stop here, however. Having the structure in place helps resident companies to upgrade.

The capacity of an economy to upgrade – its competitive potential – depends on underlying structural and institutional characteristics, such as its workforce, its infrastructure, its post-secondary educa-tional institutions, and its public policies.[9]

Porter was pitching his comments at the level of the nation. But the vitality of these characteristics can be influenced at the local level, as some of the examples in the case studies demonstrated, even if the general programme is set in train at the higher level of government.

A more strategic approach to help business to upgrade is also called for. In Rotterdam, the municipally owned port is the catalyst. Business and port managers have agreed the general approach, but details on current concerns like labour flexibility have still to find common consent. Government can come in as the broker to generate links between local industry and academic institutions, and steer research contracts to focus on specific areas. In time, an industry cluster buoyed by advanced research and development could develop, thereby, in the Porter analogy, strengthening the region's capability. The Georgia Research Alliance and the Centre for Advanced Telecommunications, concentrates not only on growth sectors but also on traditional industries like pulp and paper which can be made more environmentally acceptable. Core funding came from the state, which wanted to raise its poor image in technology and development, and from the big corporations.

Leading regions in Europe have also shown that government has a role in providing the mechanics for technology to be exchanged between business and the academic institutions. But the initiative can be on a much humbler scale, like that taken by the city of Toronto economic development officials to give an impetus to the city's development of biotechnology and biomedicine by bringing together the pharmaceuticals industry, academic and medical institutions on a regular basis.

Economic development as practised by city authorities has tended to be tied up closely with property development. Developers get a nudge with tax breaks or grants, even sometimes in the central city. In the United States this can be done on the initiative of the local government, but not in Europe or Canada where enterprise zones and grant-aid must be sanctioned at the higher level. Local government can designate industrial improvement areas, as Birmingham has done, steering private investment into them; it can kick-start development in a particular area by financing flagship buildings – museums, sports venues, conference centres, hotels and science parks.

Clear policy objectives are needed in the arena of economic development if they are to be judged on grounds of efficiency. It needs to be known whether Local Economic Initiatives are directed towards

> job creation in total, to job creation for certain groups, to job creation over a given period of time, to job creation in certain types of enterprise, or only to jobs which have a certain 'quality'. Indeed it may be that the objectives of LEIs are, instead, a parallel set of issues

relating, not to job creation, but rather to reductions in unemployment.[10]

So, is the aim of building a conference centre or baseball stadium to provide employment there and in hotels in the city? If so, will jobs be targeted on ethnic minorities, women, local residents? Or is the investment undertaken to raise the status of the city in the eyes of the nation? Does it need to make a profit which will pay interest charges on development loans, or simply meet running costs?

Birmingham's National Exhibition Centre, on the outskirts, in the adjacent borough of Solihull, has been decently profitable almost from the start, makes an annual contribution to the council's general fund, and provided the guarantee for the loans raised by the city to help finance the construction of the International Convention Centre in the central city. The NEC had raised the profile of the region rather than the city, hence the decision to take the risk of trying to repeat the process by putting the new conference centre in the city. With the airport and inter-city rail station in the vicinity, this cluster of activities helped developers to finance offices in a nearby business park which quickly rivalled the city in attracting tenants. The International Convention Centre will have a tougher job in earning its keep in the strictly financial sense.

Civic projects on this scale, however, will not be repeated in Britain, unless the private sector undertakes them. The Treasury designates borrowing by local authorities as part of total public-sector borrowing and this it is always striving to cut. Similarly, in the United States and Canada, the states and provinces, which have provided the core funding and guarantees for projects like Toronto's SkyDome and Atlanta's Georgia Dome, no longer have the resources.

The private sector is providing finance for the motorway to relieve congestion in north Birmingham and will obtain its returns from tolls. Another development is the demand that companies benefitting from a road to be built in east Birmingham have been asked to pay a proportion of the costs. In Rotterdam, developers are expected to contribute to the costs of the new bridge, and freight users to pay for part of the planned rail freight line. Partnership will mean increasingly that the private sector has to take more of the risk than in the balmier days when governments underwrote it.

The economic recovery, in theory, should create more opportunities. In practice, the private sector remains cautious. It has to be said that the implications for those cities whose infrastructure improvement plans have been squeezed out by public finance restrictions could be serious. To tell cities that they need to make better use of their resources does not obviate the need for continuing investment in the structure of those cities.

6.9 SUBJECTIVE ANALYSIS

When I told friends that I was writing a book about these four cities, they were curious to know how I would rate the cities. Which city had the best feel about it? Which would they want to live in? The questions demanded personal answers. They were not difficult to give, although with many qualifications. Toronto has the best feel for me about it, but others find its very qualities add up to dullness. Atlanta is the most stimulating, but also the most frustrating for a European who equates cities with walkable centres. Rotterdam is the most stolid, but has the most exciting physical potential from its river setting. Birmingham, where I have lived for four years, has the harshest environment but has probably tried hardest of all to reverse the planning mistakes of the 1960s. The subjective list could go on: Atlanta is aggressive, Birmingham is defensive; Rotterdam is reasonable, Toronto is pleasing.

This book set out to be objective. But inevitably the observations are tinged with some judgment. The very fascination of cities is that they provoke comment and judgment. Where once they were judged mostly by critics within their own countries, they have deliberately thrown their hats into the international ring. In this context, they might be doing something brilliantly well, but it will be those first impressions of the conference-goer and the visitor which will wing their way back home. The image will not be the reality but when cities play the competitive game they risk being judged as winners or losers. In fact, they are neither. They are survivors.

NOTES

1. Schmoke, K. (1993) *People in Cities*, SAUS Publications.
2. Stone, C. (1989) *Regime Politics*, University Press of Kansas.
3. Stein, D. L. (1993) *Going Downtown*, Oberon Press.
4. Bianchini, F. and Parkinson, M. (1993) *Cultural Policy and Urban Regeneration*, Manchester University Press.
5. Speech on the Senate floor, 26 March 1992. Edited version, *Philadelphia Inquirer*, 5 April 1992.
6. Because there is hope, *The Atlanta Project*, 1993.
7. Gardner, J. (1991) *Building Community*, Independent Sector.
8. Brian Robson (1994) At the bottom of the heap, *Guardian*, 15 June 1994.
9. Porter, M. (1991) *Canada at the Crossroads*. Paper to the Canadian Government.
10. Storey, D. (1990) Evaluation of policies and measures to create local employment, *Urban Studies*, **27**.

Index